anyone's life are:

1. We admitted we were powerless, and that our lives had become unmanageable.
2. Came to believe that a Power greater than ourselves could restore us to sanity.
3. Made a decision to turn our will and our lives over to the care of God *as we understood Him.*
4. Made a searching and fearless moral inventory of ourselves.
5. Admitted to God, to ourselves, and to another human being the exact nature of our wrongs.
6. Were entirely ready to have God remove all these defects of character.
7. Humbly asked Him to remove our shortcomings.
8. Made a list of all persons we had harmed and became willing to make amends to them all.
9. Made direct amends to such people wherever possible, except when to do so would injure them or others.
10. Continued to take personal inventory and when we were wrong promptly admitted it.
11. Sought through prayer and meditation to improve our conscious contact with God *as we understood Him,* praying only for knowledge of His will for us and the power to carry that out.
12. Having had a spiritual awakening as a result of these Steps, we tried to carry this message to others, and to practice these principles in all our affairs.

*These Twelve Steps are adapted from the Twelve Steps of Alcoholics Anonymous with permission from A.A. World Services, Inc., New York, NY.

THE TWELVE STEPS TO HAPPINESS

A handbook for all
Twelve Steppers

Joe Klaas

A Hazelden Book
BALLANTINE BOOKS • NEW YORK

To the great American ace, Gregory "Pappy" Boyington, who led me to this victory.

Copyright © 1982 by Hazelden Foundation

All rights reserved under International and Pan-American Copyright Conventions. Published in the United States by Ballantine Books, a division of Random House, Inc., New York, and simultaneously in Canada by Random House of Canada Limited, Toronto.

No part of this book may be reproduced without the written permission of the publisher.

The Twelve Steps to Happiness was originally produced as an audio cassette album by Hazelden Educational Services in 1980 and titled "The Twelve Steps: The Road to Recovery, Serenity and Happiness."

The Twelve Steps to Alcoholics Anonymous have been reprinted and adapted with the permission of A.A. World Services, Inc., New York, NY 10163.

ISBN 0-345-36787-1

This edition published by arrangement with the Hazelden Foundation

Printed in Canada

First Ballantine Books Edition: May 1990

18 17 16 15

CONTENTS

I do not conceive of God as being He, She or It. I suspect God is androgynous. I refer to God in the masculine pronoun only because centuries of usage, improper as it may be, have made it the most familiar way to communicate about our Higher Power.

—the Author

ACKNOWLEDGMENTS

The author gratefully acknowledges the Twelve Step Program of Alcoholics Anonymous and has adapted their Twelve Steps for general use with the permission of the A.A. General Services Office. The original Twelve Steps of Alcoholics Anonymous occur on pages 59 through 60 of *Alcoholics Anonymous* (the ''Big Book'')* and are as follows:

1. We admitted we were powerless over alcohol—that our lives had become unmanageable.
2. Came to believe that a Power greater than ourselves could restore us to sanity.
3. Made a decision to turn our will and our lives over to the care of God *as we understood Him*.
4. Made a searching and fearless moral inventory of ourselves.
5. Admitted to God, to ourselves, and to another human being the exact nature of our wrongs.

Alcoholics Anonymous, Third Edition, copyright 1976, published by A.A. World Services, Inc., New York, NY, pp. 59–60.

6. Were entirely ready to have God remove all these defects of character.

7. Humbly asked Him to remove our shortcomings.

8. Made a list of all persons we had harmed, and became willing to make amends to them all.

9. Made direct amends to such people wherever possible, except when to do so would injure them or others.

10. Continued to take personal inventory and when we were wrong promptly admitted it.

11. Sought through prayer and meditation to improve our conscious contact with God *as we understood Him*, praying only for knowledge of His will for us and the power to carry that out.

12. Having had a spiritual awakening as a result of these steps, we tried to carry this message to alcoholics, and to practice these principles in all our affairs.

how to live happily ever after

WOULD YOU LIKE TO BE HAPPY? Do you want to be successful? Now there is a sure-fire way to achieve both happiness and success.

Psychologists are beginning to prescribe a method of finding joy and accomplishment that has been around, but not fully recognized, for half a century. Educators are starting to teach it in schools. Pastors are preaching it to their flocks. Doctors are prescribing it to patients. Judges are even turning convicted criminals on to this new way of learning to live vastly better lives.

The tried and proven formula for attaining success is called the Twelve Steps.

Millions have found the Twelve Steps have improved their lives beyond their most optimistic aspirations. No one who has taken the magic Steps has reported negative results. All who practice them find serenity in a troubled world.

The secret of the Twelve Steps is that they are not a secret. They were not developed by psychologists, doctors or clergymen. There is no charge for them. They are free and will liberate those who take them from the bonds that hold them back.

Anyone can do the Twelve Steps. No previous training is necessary. There is only one requirement. We must be willing to go to any extreme to find happiness and success.

The first amazing fact about these Twelve simple Steps that have improved millions of lives in more than a hundred countries is that they were not discovered by scientists, theologians or philosophers. This miraculous program now enthusiastically practiced by all kinds of happy, successful people throughout the world was developed by a bunch of drunks.

It was years before it was discovered that others of us who are not alcoholics can profit almost beyond belief by only slightly modifying the same Twelve Steps.

The less than a hundred helpless heavy drinkers who inadvertently developed this gift for all humankind originally thought of the Twelve Steps only as a way for hopeless alcoholics to stop drinking. A half century of uncanny results for others who practiced the Steps proves they are much more than a way to halt addictive behavior. The Twelve Steps, adapted for general use by anyone who wants a more fulfilling life, offer a new way of living that will bring success and happiness to us all.

The second astounding thing about the Twelve Steps is that they will work for anybody and everybody.

How To Live Happily Ever After

What will adapting these Steps into our daily living accomplish for us that we cannot already do for ourselves? Let us look at areas of our lives the Twelve Steps will improve.

We will be amazed at what happens to us as we follow all twelve of these simple recommendations.

We will experience freedom and happiness we have never known before.

We will learn how to forgive ourselves and profit from past misdeeds.

We will find within ourselves a peace and serenity that will sustain us through all emergencies.

We will see ways to help others based on our own past misfortunes.

We will sense our own unique worth and no longer feel sorry for ourselves.

Selfishness will be replaced by generosity toward others.

Self-obsession will disappear.

Our values and entire approach to living will change for the better.

Other people will no longer frighten us, nor will we be afraid of running out of money.

We will learn to trust our intuition to give us the right solutions to problems we never before knew how to handle.

We will awaken to the fact that God is managing our lives better than we could for ourselves.

THE TWELVE STEPS TO HAPPINESS

Is there a risk in predicting such results? Not at all. I truly believe all these great promises will come true for anyone who diligently works all Twelve Steps to happiness. They all materialized for me. They have been fulfilled for millions of others. All these wonderful promises will happen for you if you sincerely follow the simple directions printed in the Steps.

I was first exposed to the Twelve Steps to success and happiness in 1957. I read them through, thought I easily understood them, and set about trying to practice them.

Actually nearly everything I thought I understood about the Twelve Steps was wrong. And hardly anything I did in trying to practice them was correct.

I thought of these Twelve suggested Steps only as a way to recover from a specific compulsive disease. I thought they were to be used exclusively as a means of resisting the substance or behavior I was addicted to. Not many realized in those days that these Steps would improve the lives of anyone who practiced them whether they were addicts or not.

The Steps were first published by Alcoholics Anonymous in 1939 as a program by which fewer than a hundred men and women had recovered from alcoholism. Eighteen years later when I first encountered these Steps, they were also being used by other anonymous fellowships to recover from varying diseases such as gambling, compulsive overeating, drug addiction, and by the wives, husbands and relatives afflicted with the obsession to control the behavior of family members or friends addicted to alcohol.

It was years before I realized the Twelve Steps would bring happiness and success to anyone, whether they were victims of addictions or not. In fact, the Twelve Steps suggested as a program of recovery from such diseases did not directly address those compulsive behaviors at all. Instead, the Steps presented a spiritual way of growth that made it possible to stop confronting one disease or another head on and to concentrate on living happier, more successful lives whether we suffered from addictions or not. The Steps presented a sure and miraculous nonreligious path to happiness and success in every aspect of life whether we were diseased or well.

The Twelve Steps did not *cure* any of the destructive compulsions shared in anonymous fellowships. The Steps *replaced* addictive substances or behavior as the only source of comfort for millions of distressed victims of a troubled world.

It seemed that in order to prove for all humanity a foolproof formula for success and happiness, a Higher Power had to choose degraded men and women who had sunk so low in despair and hopelessness there was no chance for them at all. He selected a bunch of drunks abandoned by nearly all who loved them and despised by those who did not. They were but the first to be given the Twelve Steps now available to us all.

For the first time in history, millions miraculously recovered from a disease for which medical science to this day has not found a cure. Twelve simple Steps had achieved what all the science, religion, philosophy, psychology and self-improvement disciplines of humankind could not accomplish.

Fifty years after these Steps were developed, I was fortunate enough to teach a Twelve Step seminar in Ohio to sixty doctors, counselors, therapists and treatment-center directors who were not themselves diseased. These professionals were wise enough from experience to realize that until they themselves learned to practice the Twelve Steps, they could not effectively treat addicted patients.

Today hundreds of terminal diseases, whether addictive or nonaddictive, have been sent into permanent remission one day at a time by the Twelve Steps. This program coincidentally discovered by a handful of helpless drunks has now enabled millions of hopeless humans, alcoholic or not, to lead joyous productive lives. Or was it coincidental? Coincidence may be God's way of remaining anonymous.

It is not a religious program. No religion is needed to practice the Twelve Steps, yet most churches now send their afflicted to Twelve Step programs. It is not a psychotherapy program, yet psychologists often prescribe the Twelve Step formula as an alternative to self-improvement. It is not morality training, yet judges send thousands to Twelve Step fellowships in lieu of jail. It works for those who are ill. They get better. It works as well for those of us who are healthy. Our lives get better, too.

I don't know why it escaped so many for so long that the Twelve Steps work as well for the healthy as they do for the diseased. They are not a medicine to wipe out the microbes of destructive addictions and compulsions. They are a way of accepting the good things in life rather than concentrating on the bad. By means of the Twelve Steps anyone, troubled or not, will live a more rewarding, happier life.

I was sick when I encountered the Twelve Steps. I was terminally ill. At the rate I was degenerating there was little time left. Doctors advised me to put my affairs in order. I didn't even know how. I was helpless. My wife dialed a telephone number for me. She suggested those at the other end might know a secret way for me to live a little longer. A warm, concerned voice on the telephone began my exposure to the Twelve Steps.

That was a third of a century ago. I plunged right in. What else could I do? I had tried medical help, religion and self-discipline. All had failed. The only thing I hadn't tried was letting go so a Higher Power could take over complete control of my failing life. No clergyman, doctor or psychologist had ever expressed such a concept. I had never before heard anyone suggest the radical idea that I could win by giving up, that the way to become healthy and improve my life was to stop being responsible and to let an Unseen Force take over.

Obviously the Twelve Steps worked for me. More than thirty healthy, prosperous and joyous years later I can assure you they did more than just keep me from dying. They gave me a long, happy and successful life more delightful, exciting and free than I could ever have imagined possible.

Will the Steps work for those who are not at Death's door? I wouldn't have thought so then. I assumed they were only for those as sick as I was. Now I know better. I haven't been sick for decades, yet through continuing the practice of this magic formula my life continues to improve beyond my wildest expectations. Each day the twilight of my years seems more like the dawn of a new life.

So, in 1957, I began to work the Steps in my own way. It wasn't the right way. But even so, working them incorrectly was better than not trying to work them at all. As much as I misunderstood them, they kept me alive and vastly improved the health and quality of my life.

I began my journey to the good life about twenty years after a bunch of losers in Ohio and New York compared twelve things they had all done to become winners. Less than 250,000 people had even heard of the Twelve Steps when I first learned of them.

Today at least three million men and women have

taken the Twelve Steps to success and happiness. In fact, these Twelve magic Steps have become the most important factor in the prosperous, joyous lives of all these people, and our numbers are increasing as thousands more learn about the miracle of the Twelve Steps. It is estimated that the number of those who latch on to this formula for happiness and success doubles every seven years. The Steps are not a religion; no religion ever caught on so fast.

For the first six years I did the Steps wrong. I clung to values I had been taught from the cradle. I still believed I was in control of my life. I thought God *expected* me to control it. I had been taught that from infancy. I simply *couldn't let go* and follow the instructions in the Steps, yet trying to do so as best I could saved my life, increased my happiness and got me in shape to take this certain way from failure to success, from despair to happiness.

The Twelve Steps have crossed continents and oceans. They are now being followed by thriving people in every country on earth, including those behind the iron curtain. The Steps were the first light from the west to penetrate the Soviet Union at the very start of *glasnost*. Today they are practiced throughout the U.S.S.R.

I was lucky enough to hear the late Lois Wilson, Al-Anon's first member and wife of A.A.'s founder, speak in 1980 at New Orleans and in 1985 at Montreal. On four separate occasions I heard her say, "I have no doubt that the principles of the

THE TWELVE STEPS TO HAPPINESS

Twelve Steps as practiced by A.A., Al-Anon, Al-Ateen, and countless others everywhere will one day bring peace to the world."

I nudged a citizen of another country sitting next to me high up in a stadium filled with 35,000 people. "But unfortunately," I mumbled, "our politicians don't practice the Twelve Steps."

"But Joe," she answered in a wonderful foreign accent. "The prime minister of my country does. He's been recovered for four years." Perhaps one day at a summit meeting heads of state will discover they all are in Twelve Step programs. World peace will have arrived at last.

"I don't know why people keep talking about the *spiritual part of our program*," Lois said far below at the podium. "The Twelve Steps *are* spiritual. That's what they are."

Six years after my first exposure to the Steps, when the number of those who had adopted these twelve simple suggestions for the best possible kind of life had nearly doubled, I began to believe the first half of the First Step. When three more years of improving life-style had passed, I was able to accept the second half of the First Step. By then, nearly a half million others, mostly people with serious problems such as overeating, gambling, dope addiction, alcoholism, or controlling addicts, had accomplished much more than miraculously arresting these grave compulsions, which they successfully did. For those who took them, the Steps almost incidentally arrested those kinds of problems while opening up a new way of living so rewarding to each individual it was hard to believe.

Everyone who took the Twelve Steps would say again and again: *"Look at me. I am a walking miracle!"* Others looked, decided to gamble on what appeared to be a sure thing and started learning how to take the tried and true Twelve suggested Steps. By 1976 there were two million, and by 1980 three million were following these Steps to life fulfillment beyond their wildest dreams. By 1990 who knows how many millions will have traveled the steady Twelve Step highway to happiness and success.

The Steps are simple. They are so simple that those of us who think of ourselves as intellectuals have the most difficulty following them. For an intellectual the shortest distance between two points is in the opposite direction all around the world with infinite exploratory side trips until hopefully what used to be the nearby destination is finally reached. That is why it took me nine years to complete the First simple Step. It need not take you that long unless you make the same mistakes I did.

Complicated people seem to have to learn the hard way what each of these simple Steps *does not mean* before they can see in plain language what they do mean. The purpose of this little book is to help you avoid the time-consuming pitfalls I stumbled through on my confused but steady way to a life that is wonderful beyond measure.

THE TWELVE STEPS TO HAPPINESS

Remember that although the magic Twelve Steps to Happiness will work for anyone at all, we got them from Bill Wilson, more affectionately remembered as Bill W., the founder of A.A. Bill first published them in A.A.'s "Big Book" in 1939. He never once suggested a dangerous bromide that floats around among doubting Thomases in various Twelve Step fellowships. Bill never at any time said, "Each person must do the Steps in his or her own way." To the contrary, the second sentence Bill wrote in the foreword to the first edition was, "To show other(s) . . . *precisely how we have recovered* is the main purpose of this book." The italics are his, not mine. *"Precisely how"* hardly told me to do the Steps my own way. I thought I'd better do precisely what they suggested, or they may not work for me precisely as they did for all those millions who were enjoying the miracle of infinitely better living than they had ever known before.

Unfortunately it is only through the process of elimination that analytical people can arrive at the new way of life spelled out in the Twelve Steps. That is because the Steps are diametrically opposed to the way our parents, teachers, preachers and employers have always taught us to conduct ourselves. Therefore, even though the language of the Steps is simple and crystal clear, we will at first persist in giving the words false meanings that conform only with what we have been taught before.

A good way for those of us with complicated

minds to find out what any one of the Steps says to do is ask a twelve-year-old to read it and tell us precisely what it suggests we do. The language of the Steps is simple enough for any adolescent to easily understand. All we have to do is what the young person tells us the Step says to do and we'll be right on.

Don't be ashamed of not quickly understanding what a Step suggests we do. Only an intellectual can misunderstand a Step. Being an intellectual is nothing to be ashamed of. Voltaire once said, "If you want to make enemies, try to change something." Before we have progressed far in the Steps, we will see that we must be willing to change. Rest assured my favorite motto will come true. "The truth will set you free, but first it will piss you off." At this juncture in the process of becoming happy and successful, we must resist the temptation not to change. We must resolve not to remain as we have always been.

It is easy to make the mistake of thinking the Steps must be done differently for different problems. What they say to do is the same for any problem. Essentially they show us a way to *let go and let God* handle the problem. Those who need to join different fellowships that address different diseases or compulsions don't have Twelve different Steps to practice in each program. They are the same Twelve Steps. Only the First and Twelfth Steps are slightly modified. In the First we admit we are powerless over some addiction or destructive behavior not properly recognized before as something we cannot control. In the Twelfth we carry the Twelve Step message to others who share that particular helplessness. Those of us already practicing the Steps in one program of recovery simply now include the heretofore unacknowledged problem in Step One, admit powerlessness over it, and include it in the Twelve Steps we are already practicing.

Do we need to go to meetings of more than one fellowship to address different diseases? Why not? We wouldn't go to a garage to get our tonsils treated, nor to a dental clinic to have a tire changed. If we already have some knowledge of the Steps, we can grow now even more by sharing the message with others suffering the same incurable ailment we at last are owning up to. The Twelve Steps to success and happiness work best for those who share them with others. But we don't do the Steps differently for different reasons. An alcoholic who has learned to give up managing his or her life in A.A. could end up getting drunk by trying to learn *control* of any different problem in another fellowship. The Twelve Steps do not allow for personal management of *any* problem. To compromise a Step we are already practicing in order to apply it to some other uncontrollable behavior would not only be illogical, it would be insane.

There are many fellowships, but there is only

one Twelve Step program. To make it work, we must share more than lip service to the Twelve Steps. We must also share the utter helplessness we need to admit in order to practice the Steps together. They cannot be done alone. There's not an *I*, or *me*, or *my* in any of the Steps.

It is not easy to give up the old ideas of right and wrong that were drilled into us from the cradle. We find it hard to abandon principles of an insane society that we have been teaching to our own children.

Truth begins when we discover we are wrong. That is the only way truth is learned. When we find out we're wrong, we can become right.

The Twelve Steps, if we let them, will cleanse our minds of all we have previously been taught about how to live. They will let us start again as we were created at the beginning of learning. These Twelve Steps will show us how to be reborn. After rebirth they will make our lives successful.

Success is to do what you want to do. Failure is to not do it.

The first words our mothers taught us were, "No no. Naughty naughty. Baby mustn't do that." And what was going on when she said "Naughty naughty"? Probably something as normal and reasonable as crying, wetting our diaper or letting food run down our faces because we hadn't yet learned it's more comfortable to not do those things. And mamma said, "No no. Naughty baby mustn't do

17

that!'' Soon our daddies, uncles and aunts, and older brothers and sisters were saying, ''No no. Bad baby!'' No matter what we wanted to do, particularly if it felt good, the neighbors, teachers, cops on the beat, preachers and playground supervisors all said *no* to us. When we reached that magic age of puberty and there were even more normal things we could enjoy, we were not only told, ''No, no, naughty baby!'', our trainers grew angry with us and shouted, ''It's time you grew up! Being grown up means we shouldn't have to say *no* to you all the time. Growing up means you've got to say *no* to yourself!''

And so we were taught from the cradle to turn ourselves down, to say *no no, baby* to ourselves, particularly when we wanted to do something natural.

If success is doing what you feel like doing and failure is not doing it, then we spent our lives teaching ourselves to be failures. Instead of learning how to say yes to ourselves, we were trained to turn ourselves down. We were taught to practice failure. Yet in middle years we will look into a mirror and ask ''Why aren't you a success?'' What chance do we have of succeeding in a society that teaches us to say no to ourselves over and over.

Isn't it true that during that split second of opportunity that catches us by surprise, our instincts have been trained either to say *no* immediately or to deliberate about the opportunity until it is too late to do anything? By then any chance at success will have long passed us by.

The Twelve Steps will teach you to say *yes* to yourself. *Yes* all the time. When you can say yes you will be a success.

These Steps will enable you to live without fear, guilt or worry. When you can do that you will be happy.

The Twelve Steps are not religious, although six of them will put you in direct contact with a loving God you are not required to understand. When you have completed all Twelve Steps you will no longer blindly *believe* in God. Belief is a substitute for knowledge. Through the Twelve Steps you will *experience* God. God will be proven at last. Religion will not be necessary for this miracle to happen. You need no religion to take the Twelve Steps to happiness and prosperity.

You need neither deserve nor earn the good life. All you have to do is want it, take the Twelve Steps and accept the best of living. The further away from well-being you have drifted, the easier it may be to take the Steps. For some, it will be necessary to sink to ultimate depths of fear, failure and despair to take even the First Step. Others willing to gamble their very lives on the totally Unknown need not descend so far to start the Steps. And those sitting pretty, who are willing to let go and "let God" by working these Steps, will find themselves sitting even prettier.

THE TWELVE STEPS TO HAPPINESS

All Twelve Steps cannot be completed in a day, a week, a month or a year. Some may never be completed at all. It will take a long time, one day at a time, but the journey will not be tedious. No amount of willpower will speed your way through the Twelve Steps. Yet all your willpower may be required to take the First Step or to move from one Step to another. But the positive results of trying to take the Steps will brighten your life from the very beginning. Life will get better and continue to improve as long as you try to take the Steps. Or, anywhere along the line to happiness you can abandon the Twelve Steps, and your misery will be refunded.

You may think you have taken Step One, or Step Three, or Step Eight many times, and later learn that you had only thought you had taken it without really having done so. But you always get another chance, and another, until finally you have taken each Step.

You will see shortcuts, but there really are none. No easier, softer way to success and happiness exists. You may come to believe there is no other way at all. It may become obvious that from the beginning of time no one ever fully became successful and happy without either deliberately, instinctively or accidentally following the principles of the Twelve Steps.

This adaptation of the Twelve Steps which will vastly improve anyone's life are:

How To Live Happily Ever After

1. We admitted we were powerless, and that our lives had become unmanageable.
2. Came to believe that a Power greater than ourselves could restore us to sanity.
3. Made a decision to turn our will and our lives over to the care of God *as we understood Him.*
4. Made a searching and fearless moral inventory of ourselves.
5. Admitted to God, to ourselves, and to another human being, the exact nature of our wrongs.
6. Were entirely ready to have God remove all these defects of character.
7. Humbly asked Him to remove our shortcomings.
8. Made a list of all persons we had harmed and became willing to make amends to them all.
9. Made direct amends to such people wherever possible, except when to do so would injure them or others.
10. Continued to take personal inventory and when we were wrong promptly admitted it.
11. Sought through prayer and meditation to improve our conscious contact with God as we understood Him, praying only for knowledge of His will for us and the power to carry that out.
12. Having had a spiritual awakening as the result of these Steps, we tried to carry this message to others, and to practice these principles in all our affairs.

THE TWELVE STEPS TO HAPPINESS

The first time I read these Steps I said, "Wonderful. I agree with all that. I already live that way. I learned it in church." Wrong. The Steps are not what I learned in church. There I learned to pray for God to help me attain goals I had already decided upon. I asked Him only for specific things, and as far as living my life was concerned, I only prayed for Him to help me manage it. That is not the magic way of the Twelve Steps to happiness.

A pitfall awaits us the first time we read the Twelve Steps. Many of us think they repeat what we have learned in other places, such as in religion, psychology, philosophy or in some school of mind over matter that teaches us how to accomplish our own goals by visualization, the power of positive thought, mind control, placing the adult in us in charge of the child in us, learning to love ourselves, setting boundaries, awakening the third eye, predetermining what is acceptable or unacceptable behavior, or centering ourselves in the universe. We may have found such techniques useful in trying to manage our lives, but none of them is anything like the Twelve Steps. The moment we adopt some additional method of changing, controlling or managing behavior, we are trying to exert human power over unmanageable lives. We are trying to manage. We are renouncing the Steps in favor of some other well-intentioned program. There is no objection to anyone trying any or all of these other techniques of self-improvement.

However, we must acknowledge that such methods of accomplishing human goals are not compatible with the Steps. They make practicing the Twelve Steps impossible.

The choice is ours. Are we going to do the Twelve Steps or something else? It's up to us.

If you think you recognize in the Twelve Steps a way of life you have learned somewhere else, you are mistaken. Read on before deciding the way of the Steps is already yours. In fact, the Steps will turn you on to a new way of reaching success and happiness that is probably 180 degrees opposite anything you think they resemble, and totally unlike any way to triumph over life that you have ever heard of before.

Remember, the truth will set you free, but at first it may annoy the daylights out of you. Changing one's way of life may be easy with the Twelve Steps, but choosing to change is not easy at all.

Using the Steps that teach us to give up control of our lives as a means of sharpening such control is absurd. Letting go and "letting God" is not hanging on and doing it ourselves. "Letting God" is not asking Him to help us do it. It is asking Him to do it for us.

The Steps are simple. Deciding to take them and paying strict attention to what they actually say are difficult. Living the way we have been taught all our lives may not be pleasant, but it is comfortable to follow orders. Deciding to embark on an entirely new way of life is not comfortable, although the new life may be easier.

It is like prayer. It is not difficult to pray the way we have been taught all our lives. It may take all the determination we can muster to abandon our old habits and adopt an entirely different way to pray, a way of prayer we have heard of all our lives, but which we have never tried before. The old way was easy but ineffective. The new way will be hard at first, but it will work every time.

Part of a prayer first introduced to the United States by a New England theologian may be useful until you learn how to take the First Step. I once saw this portion of the prayer ascribed to St. Francis of Assisi on a plaque for sale in a religious gift shop. I am happy for this opportunity to correct the record. The entire nonsectarian prayer, the first sentence of which is used to open nearly every Twelve Step meeting in the world, was first invoked in 1926 by Reinhold Niebuhr.

*God, grant me the serenity to
accept the things I cannot change,
courage to change the things I
can, and wisdom to know the
difference.*

*Living one day at a time, accepting
hardships as the pathway to peace,*

*taking as He did, this world as it
is, not as I would have it.*

*Trusting that He will make all
things right if I surrender to His
will, that I may be reasonably
happy in this life and supremely
happy with Him, forever, in the
next.*

Even though the second verse of the above in-
vocation prayed eleven years before A.A. or any
other Twelve Step fellowship was founded provides
in its second verse the concept of acceptance and
"living one day at a time," only the first part of
the prayer has been adapted by those who share the
Twelve Steps everywhere. It is a better method of
living than most of us are used to, a formula for
managing our lives as best we can until we become
convinced wc cannot manage them at all. It is like
a first aid kit, something to use to stay alive until
the doctor comes. We call it The Serenity Prayer.

*God grant me the serenity
To accept the things I cannot change,
The courage to change the things I can,
And the wisdom to know the difference.*

It is the best way ever devised for anyone who
still believes he must manage his or her own life
to temporarily continue to try to do so.

THE TWELVE STEPS TO HAPPINESS

The Serenity Prayer alone has worked miracles in people's lives. But remember The Serenity Prayer comes before the First Step. It is not a substitute for any of the Steps and will not bring anything like the success and happiness the Twelve Steps will bring you.

Use this prayer often at first, especially in moments of strife or anxiety. It will bring you the peace needed before you can logically proceed with the miraculous adventure of taking the Twelve suggested Steps to success and happiness.

This is not a religious program, but it definitely involves you with God, whether as you understand Him or don't understand Him. If you are atheistic or agnostic, don't let it dissuade you. The universe itself, or nature or the laws of physics may be your Higher Power. Some who have difficulty adjusting to the word *God* add an *o* to it and substitute the word *Good* in the Twelve Steps.

Anyone can take the Twelve Steps. Your back need not be against the wall. All you need to take them is a desire to be happier and more successful than you are now.

The Steps are numbered One through Twelve. The purpose of calling them Steps is to let us know that we move up them one after another just as we would any other flight of steps. Or in the same way a baby learns to walk one step at a time. Obviously the purpose of putting numbers in front of them is to let us know the order in which to initially take them as we begin this journey of adventure toward a life full of rewards.

We start with Step One and do each Step individually in progression up through number Twelve. It will require lots of time and effort. Once we have progressed through all Twelve Steps to a spiritual awakening we have never before experienced, we will learn to apply the Steps selectively to whatever situations come up in daily living. We will be able to choose whatever Step we need take again at any time to let a Power greater than ourselves manage our thoughts, emotions and behavior and see us through any trouble or obstacle we run up against.

The Steps do not prevent bad things from happening. They provide the serenity to survive with calmness and grace any unpleasantness that may befall us. They will give us the cool heads we need to get through any good or bad situation without falling apart. Our intuition will be sharpened by a Higher Power so we can trust it to inspire the proper moves to get us beyond disaster.

The Steps provide serenity as a firm foundation upon which to build a better life. Without turmoil now and then, serenity would be useless. If nothing ever went wrong we wouldn't need serenity. How would we know if we had serenity without troubles to use it on? Success and happiness are not reached by denying we have difficulties. We arrive at success and happiness by surrounding difficulties.

Some of us go to pieces when things go "too

well.'' We actually fear success. The Steps replace that fear with serenity. We no longer fear success. We get used to it. We grow to love it. Success makes us happy and attractive. We become winners at last. Others like to be around us because we have something wondrous to share. Our Twelve Step way of life grows as we give it away. We carry its message. The more we spread it around, the happier we become. Its pitcher is so full of joy that the more we pour from it the fuller it gets.

If you still think these Steps, originally developed by alcoholics only to recover from insane drinking, won't improve your healthy life, think a minute about how they performed the miracle of recovery for those less fortunate than you. First, they have provided total remission of the incurable disease of Alcoholism to more than two million members of A.A. The Steps present by far the most successful way for incurable drug addicts to recover. Incurable gamblers overcome their compulsion with the Twelve Steps. Compulsive overeaters who have failed to solve their problem by any known diet plan return to sane eating habits by means of these Steps. They enable nicotine addicts who never before were able to stop smoking to knock off cigarettes forever, one day at a time. They enable compulsive debtors to spend sanely and accumulate wealth. The unconquerable disease of co-dependence is subdued by the Twelve Steps.

People diagnosed with terminal cancer, AIDS and other deadly diseases survive with the Steps.

"Wait a minute!" someone will shout. "AIDS? Cancer?" The doubter's head will shake. "The Steps won't work for a virus or malignancy. Those illnesses are incurable." That's what the Steps originally were for. An incurable disease. Alcoholism is incurable. So is compulsive gambling or overeating. Medical science has not yet found a satisfactory way to address the world's drug problem, except to beg patients to *"get into a Twelve Step program."* The Steps enable the afflicted to survive incurable diseases, not by science or logic, but by *miraculous* recovery. The Power greater than ourselves that makes these Steps work is not a man-made Power. It is not a rational Power. It is a *supernatural* Power greater than ourselves.

I used to wonder why it took me so long to see the logic of the Twelve Steps. Once I saw the logic, I wondered why others steeped in logic couldn't see it too. Only by watching others with training in logic flounder with the Steps did I finally understand the difficulty intellectuals trained in logic had in comprehending them. The fact is, the Steps aren't logical. This path to a life of happiness and success is not a logical procedure. It requires us to "come to believe" that a supernatural Force greater than all mankind will make us happy, joyous and free. Nothing supernatural is logical. The Twelve Steps produce a certifiable miracle that works to better our lives. A miracle by definition is not logical. That is why it is called a miracle.

As a child I wished I could have lived in the wondrous time of biblical miracles. I always wished I could see one. I practiced the Twelve Steps for years before it dawned on me that I have seen thousands of miracles, more miracles than are related in all the bibles of the world. I had seen so many that I was taking miracles for granted.

The miracle of the Twelve Steps requires faith. Fortunately the Steps themselves create the faith that's needed. By watching these Steps work in others and feeling them work for us, even those most doubting are moved beyond rationalism to grow and be blessed by the Steps. They become logical only as we begin to believe in them.

The Twelve Steps are the formula for what the great psychiatrist, Carl Gustaf Jung, described in a letter dated January 30, 1961, to Bill W. as "a higher education of the mind beyond the confines of mere rationalism." There is no need to have a detailed understanding of God to bring us success and happiness. Those drunks who first laid out the Steps for us in 1939 called the Higher Power *"God as we understood Him."* The only understanding they could agree on was that God was *"a Power greater than ourselves."* It is still the only understanding we need.

The Twelve Step road to success and happiness is not a pragmatic approach to life. It leads "beyond the confines of mere rationalism." It is a spiritual program that is in its second half century of proving beyond doubt that "a Power greater than ourselves" succeeds where no human power can.

Perhaps if we still think the Twelve Steps, which put only that Higher Power to work on our problems, will not work for AIDS or cancer, we ought to take an inventory of what other aspects of human life we think would be too much for God. God can't handle a virus? Or a malignancy? Come *on*. What else can God not handle? What other things are more powerful than God?

If you are skeptical, good. Those of insufficient faith will find it as they progress through the Steps. Step One requires no reliance on a Higher Power. It requires only lack of faith in human power. It requires lack of confidence in ourselves. Not a total lack of self-sufficiency, but a very human doubt that we can live up to our full potential without first discovering a better formula than we now have for achieving maximum success.

The point is that if the Twelve Steps will work for those who suffer incurable diseases or unconquerable self-destructive compulsions, or for those who have descended to the depths of depression or poverty, why wouldn't they work to bring about a better life for someone like you who does not have such dire problems?

Rest assured, those who practice the Steps do not remain for long at the bottom of despair. I personally have witnessed almost daily the miracle right before my eyes. I have seen the impoverished prosper, the terminal cancer go into remission, the HIV positive person survive without contracting AIDS, the heavy smoker never smoke again, the homebound agoraphobic (fear of the marketplace) attending concerts and shopping in supermarkets, the drug-free former crack user pumping iron in the gym. Because I have been blessed to deliver this message to such hopeless people and have watched them miraculously recover from dire troubles beyond man-made solutions doesn't mean I should expect you to jump right in and take the same Steps to an even better life that they took to escape from hell. That will be entirely up to you.

But if it works for them, why wouldn't it work for you?

There's a choice to be made by those of us fortunate enough to be exposed to the Twelve Steps. There's no need to wait for the elevator to reach the bottom. We can get off at any floor. Or we can enter it going up and ride to the top of our lives.

If you are willing to go to any lengths to receive what millions of sensationally revitalized people have already received through taking the Twelve suggested Steps, you are ready to turn the page and take a long look at Step One.

step one

We admitted we were powerless, and that our lives had become unmanageable.

IT MAY OR MAY NOT BE EASY TO SAY *I admit I am powerless*. But even if we can say it, we may not believe it. And if we do not believe we are powerless, merely saying *I admit I am powerless* will not really be admitting it. It will be mouthing something we don't believe. In fact, isn't it really impossible for us to admit to anything we do not know is true?

Who wants to admit he possesses no power at all? Our society teaches us to seek power. The most respected persons in the community are usually the heads of corporations, high-ranking military officers, powerful politicians, strong religious leaders, champion athletes. We were taught, and we teach our children, to try and be powerful members of the community. Most parents would be proud to have their offspring grow up to be president of the United States, or of General Motors, or a doctor ruling a large hospital with an iron fist for the good of mankind. If we say *I admit I am powerless* are we not owning up to total failure in the eyes of our families, friends and peers? Besides, who says we should admit to weakness we don't believe?

No one says it. The first part of the First Step says *we admitted we were powerless*. It doesn't suggest we lie about it if we don't believe we are powerless. To admit we are powerless we have to truly be powerless, and we have to know we are powerless.

Alcoholics who first took this Step had learned the hard way that they were powerless over alcohol. Narcotics addicts who took this path to recovery were convinced they were powerless over drugs. Overweight people who worked the Steps had realized they were powerless over compulsive overeating. As obvious as their complete lack of power over these things were, they had great difficulty in accepting their true states of powerlessness. In fact, only an extremely small minority of those afflicted with compulsive overeating, drug addiction, alcoholism, schizophrenia, neuroses, compulsive gambling, habitual smoking, chronic child beating and other self-destructive maladies ever recognize they have these problems, let alone admit they are powerless over them.

Yet anyone who searches his own life and inner self must certainly come upon something he is powerless over. A farmer is powerless over the weather. A businessman is powerless over national and world economy. The cancer victim and future cancer victim are powerless over cancer. Everyone is powerless over the behavior of others and even most of his own behavior. Two certain formulae for failure are to try and behave exactly the way someone else wants us to behave or to get others to behave the way we want them to. Both are impossible. Attempts to accomplish these kinds of controls over behavior have led to wars and genocide for thousands of years.

Apparently we are powerless over politics. Some of us are powerless over poverty, or disease, or earthquakes, or floods, or world affairs, or accidents, or love.

But today, as in all times, there are so-called "awareness level raising" programs fanatically involving millions of people with the false premise that each individual is personally responsible for everything that happens to him. Those who believe they must continue to take full responsibility for everything that happens to them cannot possibly admit they are powerless. You can't be powerless and be responsible too. It's impossible. So those trained to assume responsibility for everything in their lives will have to give up that old idea, as new as it may seem in an "awareness level raising" package, in order to take even the first half of the First Step.

We admitted we were powerless. Can we do that without offending God? Didn't He give us brains, muscles and talent to go forth and work hard and be responsible citizens? Or did He instead say to man and woman, *you have partaken of the forbidden fruit of the tree of knowledge and learned how to provide for yourself against My wishes? All right. If you think you are so smart, get out of My garden and run your own lives! And don't come back until you have learned some manners and are willing to let Me be responsible again!*

Did God give us talent and will to take over our own lives, or did He throw us out of Eden for having usurped His responsibility? One of the biggest barriers to taking the First Step will be overcome if we can get rid of the idea that God expects us to take the credit or blame for everything good or bad that happens to us. That we are powerless over our own lives and the lives of others is a truth we must arrive at either by logic or by bitter experience. Logic is the easy way to learn we are powerless. Bitter experience is the hard way and will be no fun at all.

A man gasping his last breath under a wall that, without warning, has fallen to crush him will know he is powerless. A mother pressing to her bosom the body of a child run over by a truck will know she is powerless. A pilot plunging earthward in a burning airliner with 240 passengers aboard will know the meaning of powerlessness, and so will his passengers. They will have taken the first half of the First Step, but there won't be much time left to take the rest.

Step One

With our backs against a wall facing death or ruin, it is not difficult to admit we are powerless. But with three square meals a day to nurture us, two cars in the garage and plenty of credit cards in our wallets, it is more human to take credit for the good things that come our way and blame others for the bad.

For a thousand bloody years, noblemen of northern Europe sought the Holy Grail. The Grail was not a cup passed around at The Last Supper, a meaning given to it in the fairy-tale versions of Camelot. The Grail was the heart of a man, and it became a chalice to receive the power of God only if his brain or ego could be gotten out of the way. To find the Grail, a knight was required to embark on spiritual quests. Nine times, in selfless service without possibility of reward, the nobleman was required to place himself in such dire jeopardy that he could no longer save his own life. Only God could step in to prevent certain death. Even in those days when knights were bold and superstition flourished, God had to save man from extinction nine times before his ego could be set aside to let the ray of God pass down through the crown into the heart. Then and only then could God rule through man.

The only way knights of old could conceive to place themselves in jeopardy nine times was in war. To avoid war with other Christians, they invaded the Middle East and slaughtered "heathens" for a thousand years for no other purpose than to provoke retaliation, place themselves in great danger, and be rescued nine times by God to make them fit to rule their less enlightened brethren in His name.

The spiritual awakening in finding the Grail was in being convinced at last that God really was more competent in an emergency than the individual. Or to reverse it, that man alone is really without power, or is powerless.

All you have to do to convince yourself that you are powerless is set a goal with all its rewards specified in detail. You will never achieve it exactly as you set out to do. Even if you come close, you will never accomplish anything exactly the way you planned, nor will your achievement include all the details you expect. The joy of even partly attaining such a goal will be diluted by the frustrating way of life required to try to accomplish a goal. People who set goals live in the past when they set them and in the future when they hope to attain them. They forget how to live in the now at all. So by the time they get to any goal, they have already superimposed another goal upon it and, therefore, never arrive satisfied at a destination.

It is impossible to proceed with the second half of the First Step unless you learn first to live only in the present, one day at a time, with no goals at all. For the second half of the First Step is to *admit that our lives have become unmanageable*. How could we possibly plan ahead enough to achieve goals unless we are planning our own future? In other words, he who plans goals is obviously still trying to manage his life. As long as we think we can do that, we will be unable to admit we cannot.

Once again, facing up to the admission that we cannot manage our own lives, we must arrive at knowledge that is diametrically opposed to everything we have previously been taught. Have we not been told by preachers, teachers, and beloved parents that the way to success and happiness is to efficiently manage our own lives? And is it not drummed into us that the really successful person is one who manages not only his own life, but as many other lives as possible? If he manages several, he is a boss, and what greater goal can there be, according to our mentors, than to manage our lives well enough to become bosses? If we can manage several hundred thousand lives, we may become mayor or president of a labor union. If we can manage a couple-of-hundred million lives, we may become President of the United States or Prime Minister of Great Britain. But if we cannot even manage our own lives, what chance is there for us to achieve success?

The answer is none. There is no way we can *achieve* success if we cannot learn to manage our lives. But we can *accept* success if it comes to us from outside of ourselves. Yet before we can even consider accepting a fate determined by such an outside force, we must somehow have it irrefutably proven that indeed *our lives have become unmanageable* and that we will never learn how to manage them.

Most of us would never be able to get support for such a doctrine from our parents, employers, teachers, preachers or commanding officers. No judge or jury is apt to agree that there is no use for you to keep on trying to manage your life. The only way you can come to admit that your life is unmanageable is to discover once and for all that managing it is impossible. In other words you have to *know* your life is unmanageable before you can admit it.

How can you come to know that? Well, take a look at how your life has been going so far. Has it been going the way you want it to? If it has, there is no need to take the Twelve Steps. You are probably instinctively living according to the principles of the Steps, or you wouldn't be so satisfied with your life.

But perhaps you are not completely satisfied with the way things have been going lately, or for most of your life if you think about it. Yet have you not, for the most part, been trying to manage your life the best way you know how? Then why isn't life progressing exactly the way you planned it? Could it be that no matter how hard you try to manage your life, you really don't know how?

We are apt to say *that is ridiculous. I know the*

difference between right and wrong, because I have had good parents, teachers and ministers show me from childhood what is right and what is wrong. All I have to do to manage my life is do what is right and not do what is wrong. Anyone who knows the difference between right and wrong should be able to manage his own life by following the rules.

But what rules? The rules of the United States or of Soviet Russia? The rules of the Puritans or of the liberated generations? Do we follow the rules of Mohammed, Lenin, the Pope, Yogananda, the Supreme Court, Hitler or Moses? Or do we just do what our mama tells us and not do anything she wouldn't approve of? Perhaps we should just do what our employers tell us for fifty years and get a gold watch for managing our lives so well. But will a gold watch mean we are successful? Or we could make up our own rules with advice of legal counsel, influence legislators to bend the rules to our own business needs and have a key to the washroom, high blood pressure and ulcers to prove we managed our way to the top.

Sooner or later upon close examination, we must conclude that no matter what we thought we were doing while trying to manage our lives, the results were never quite what we planned, nor as rewarding as we expected. We will one day find ourselves nodding wistfully to the music of Peggy Lee singing *Is this all there is?*

If it is not too late, we will realize we never

really possessed the talent to manage our lives at all. What we had was a mistaken belief not only that we could, but that we must. We thought it was our duty, and that arriving in positions of power over others proved we had done our duty well. But, hopefully, we will finally know we managed nothing. What we did was alter the plans of a much better Manager. We were powerless to manage our lives, no matter what we had been taught by others who were as ignorant about life as we were.

And when we finally know that *we are powerless and that our lives have become unmanageable,* then and only then can we get on with the business of admitting it. When we do that, we probably will say, *I have taken the first of the Twelve Steps.*

But have we? We could not decide to admit we were powerless. It had to be proven to us. Only after we knew it, could we admit it. We did not decide our lives were unmanageable. It became obvious that not only were we unable to manage our lives, but that no one else seemed to be able to do it either. Then and only then, with true humility of absolute knowledge that we and all mankind are totally incompetent of self management, we were able to admit it about ourselves. We did not take the First Step at all. It was the other way around. The First Step finally took us.

A sense of relief immediately comes over us. If we are powerless and cannot manage our lives, then we no longer have to take the blame for our mistakes, unless we continue to try to manage our own lives. If we continue to try, having admitted we cannot, we must be insane. Only an insane person would, day after day, continue to try to do something he knows is impossible.

But if it is useless to try to manage our lives, because it is impossible, then what are we to do instead? It is very well to discover and be able to admit our lives are unmanageable, but after a lifetime dedicated to trying to manage ourselves, what are we to do instead?

The First Step does not answer this question. It must be time to move on to Step Two.

step two

Came to believe that a Power greater than ourselves could restore us to sanity.

NOW THERE'S AN IDEA THAT CAN make the piecemeal experimenter move right along to another Step. Those who think they need only work the Steps they believe apply to themselves may try to casually pass the Second Step by.

How can we be restored to sanity unless we are insane?

I've never been in a padded cell, nor in a mental hospital, nor even been treated by a psychiatrist, we may rationalize. *Therefore, this Step does not apply to me.* Step Two is obviously a good Step, but only for those who are insane.

That is correct. Step Two is for the insane. But before we rule ourselves out of that category, let us reexamine how rational we really are.

The first words we ever understood on this earth were, "No, no"; "No no, baby, mustn't do that." And what was it we were doing? Something natural like drooling or urinating or moving our bowels. It was assumed that if we were allowed to do these things the natural ways babies do them, we would grow up drooling, urinating and moving our bowels baby fashion throughout our lives. We were not even given the opportunity to discover more comfortable ways of functioning on our own as we grew into adults.

But those were only the first "no no's" in our development toward model citizenship. Soon our fathers were saying "no no" to us as were our brothers and sisters. Then neighbors and relatives joined in to tell us what not to do, followed by Sunday school and public school teachers, preachers, doctors and cops on the beat. Everyone kept saying *no* whenever we started to do anything we wanted to all the years we were growing up. When we reached puberty and there were even more natural things to do, not only were we told "no no," but the adults around us would become angry with us.

"You are getting mature now," they would shout. "We shouldn't have to keep saying *no* to you anymore. You must learn to say *no* to yourself."

So for the rest of our lives we are trained to turn ourselves down. Remember the definition of success? *Success is to do what you want to do. Failure is to not do what you want to do.* By constantly turning ourselves down we are practicing failure all our lives. Is it sane behavior to practice failure for our entire existence on this earth?

"But I'm only following the rules of society," we insist. "People can't run around doing what they want to do. That would be anarchy."

And who made the rules of society? Ostensibly in western society, the rules are based on Moses' Ten Commandments. But there are more than ten rules. The Commandments Moses brought down from the mountain, to get his people moving again from where they would surely perish in the desert, were amended as soon as they arrived in the promised land. The First Commandment to be amended was *Thou shalt not kill.* It was amended when The Chosen were attacked by the unchosen. *Thou shalt not kill* was changed to *Thou shalt not kill except in war. Then thou shalt kill in the name of God.*

Changes in the Ten Commandments have been taking place ever since. Law libraries of Judaic-Christian nations bulge with amendments to the Ten Commandments. Presumably the ten simple laws God gave to Moses were not enough for humans who quickly set about to improve them. And humans have been improving them ever since. New laws by the thousands are passed each year in every nation on earth. Non-Judaic-Christian nations modify and increase their rules annually just as the amenders of the Ten Commandments do.

This is not an indictment of the Ten Commandments which serve a myriad of religions based on them. But remember, the Twelve Steps are difficult enough to follow without confusing them with Ten

Commandments mankind has never succeeded in obeying.

To take Step Two we must first be insane. A dictionary definition of insanity is—*to exhibit or be afflicted with mental disorder.* A legal definition of insanity is—*to be unable to distinguish between right and wrong.* We may not feel we qualify as insane according to the dictionary. After all, are we really afflicted with mental disorder? But how about the legal definition of insanity? Do we really know the difference between right and wrong?

"Of course," we may instantly reply. "Any fool who has been taught from childhood what is right and what is wrong certainly should be able to tell the difference." And anyone who can distinguish between right and wrong ought to be able to conduct himself responsibly by doing only what is right and never doing what is wrong. Do you know anyone like that?

Then what about the First Step? Did we not learn in the First Step that our lives were unmanageable? Well if we know the difference between right and wrong and only have to do the right things and not do the wrong things to lead exemplary lives, then why can't we manage our lives?

The only logical answer must be, that since we cannot manage our own lives, it must be because we only think we know what is right and what is wrong.

But what about the rules printed in the written

word of God? Thousands of years ago an inordinately clever man arose one morning and told his neighbor, ''God came to see me last night and told me to tell you what to do and not to do.''

''He did?'' responded the impressed neighbor. ''You mean all I have to do to get to Heaven is do what you tell me from now on and not do what you tell me not to do?''

''That's what God told me to tell you,'' replied the man, who thereby became a king.

It was a great relief for the neighbor, because now all he had to do to get along was follow rules laid down by the king in the name of God.

But the king grew old and called his first-born son to a conference. ''Son,'' he said, ''I am going to die soon. Since my first conversation with God, I have accumulated a lot of real estate, great wealth, and power over people. I keep all this merely by passing along the rules of God. When I die, you'd better start doing the same.''

''But, Dad,'' the son replied. ''How can I do that unless God talks to me, too, as He did with you?''

''Son,'' said the king, ''you'd better start having conversations with God or the people will take all this real estate, wealth and power away from you. They might even kill you.''

From that day on, each succeeding king passed along the word of God and kept his kingdom growing until finally some rebellious intellectuals objected.

"I don't think he is having conversations with God at all," a rebel would say.

"I don't think so either," another would agree. "Let's kill the king."

They did, and guess who replaced the king in handing down the rules of God? Fifty-one percent of the voters? Perhaps anyone who could believe that is insane.

It is at least doubtful from the beginning of time until the present that God ever told one person to tell another what to do or not to do. But, perhaps He will tell you what to do with your own life if you stop listening to mortal rulers and listen to God.

Civilizations of the world are run according to mankind's rules enforced either in the name of God or in the name of the people. How well is this system running?

We can only be sane by following the rules if the rules are right. We can only tell the difference between right and wrong, according to these rules, if the society which created them knows the difference between right and wrong. If society is run on correct principles of right and wrong, then what is going on out there?

We live in a society which, in this century, has seen millions of people slaughtered in warfare, millions more gassed and cremated to *purify the human race*, millions discriminated against on the basis of race or religion, and millions more stricken by cancer and respiratory diseases from breathing air polluted by science and industry. We see often-interrupted peace maintained only because world powers keep nuclear missiles that when fired may incinerate all living creatures from this planet. We live in a society so restrictive that we are taught to drink, smoke, ingest or inject mind-altering chemicals or drugs in order to achieve temporary freedom to do the things *we want to do* instead of what our rulemakers tell us *we ought to do*. We are products of a world in which it is believed *normal* to alter our minds with alcohol or drugs and *abnormal* not to.

If the world is sane, why isn't it operating better? Obviously the whole world is crazy. It is mad as a hatter, and anyone who hopes to be restored to sanity must be prepared to become a member of an extremely small minority. Most of humankind has become as insane as the society we are trained from birth to conform to.

To obey all the rules of a system which results in a billion people going hungry and millions starving to death while a billion or so take for granted the expenditure of fifty dollars or more on dinner for two is certainly not an indication of total sanity. Those of us who hope to be returned to sanity by taking the Twelve Steps had better be prepared to accept the position that all the world is out of step but us. Society is obviously stark raving mad. Because we have been the products of this lunatic system, we too are as looney as the world we squirm in.

Since we have been doing everything we could to behave like our insane neighbors all our lives, have we ever been sane? To come *to believe that a Power greater than ourselves* can restore us to sanity presupposes that *at one time we must have been sane.*

But when could that have been? It must have been before we were trained to believe responsibility and maturity mean to regularly and dutifully say *no* to ourselves. That must have been sometime after we left our mother's wombs, but before she started saying "no no baby" to stop us from doing perfectly natural things. It must have been when we were still what a Higher Power had created us to be, yet before man got hold of us to reshape us in the ways of a society that any fool can see hasn't been working very well.

In other words, we were sane when we were born, but not long after that. Our parents meant well when they reshaped us with the help of all those teachers, preachers and legislators into something other than what our Creator had in mind. We became afraid to look strangers in the eye for more than a second or two before looking the other way. We became afraid to smile at people for very long unless we had been introduced. We avoided sitting down beside attractive strangers on buses, if we could possibly locate a double empty seat. To socialize with people, we found it necessary to smoke or drink something *to break the ice*. We became unable to behave with freedom and do the things we wanted to, instead of what we ought to, without turning to a *higher power* that came in a joint or a bottle. The bitter truth is that we drank or used drugs to escape the unnatural restrictions of a so-called free society. Without temporary sanity which came in a cocktail glass or some other artificial form, most of us never learned to be human at all. Some of us found escape in eating too much, which gave us a false sense of security. Others became neurotic, self-pitying, rebellious or resigned to mediocrity among equally well-conditioned masses who compromised all natural instincts to remain safely hidden in a threatening civilization. Many became compulsively sexual, finding only in a few seconds of orgasm that temporary escape from the discomfort of living by man-made rules.

We all sought to sublimate our unhappy restlessness in powers higher than ourselves such as food, sex, drugs, booze, self-pity, aggression, crime, marriage, school, gambling, religion, music, entertainment, sleep, business or by simply hiding in hopes of escaping all embarrassment and pain. Some even withdrew into mental hospitals or suicide *to get away from it all*.

THE TWELVE STEPS TO HAPPINESS

So the idea of going to a power higher than ourselves for comfort and freedom is not new to us. But the concept that what we are really trying to do by resorting to these temporary means of escape is to return for brief periods to sanity is a new one. That we are seeking temporarily to become relaxed, friendly, self-confident human beings the way our Creator intended cannot be that difficult to believe. The problem is that we are seeking sanity in a bottle or a beefsteak with plenty of mashed potatoes, or insecure dependence upon other people, or in drugs or oblivion, or some other passing power greater than ourselves, instead of turning to the Highest Power available to all.

Suffice it to say we must be convinced no amount of effort on our own will return us to our natural state. Then the logical conclusion is that only a Power Greater Than Ourselves will stand a chance of returning us to a new beginning unimpaired by the unnatural conditioning of a mad, mad world.

Only the Power which created the drooling and squalling infant could restore us, fully-grown, to the newborn state of consciousness before *no* became the first word we learned. Only our Creator, or Nature, or the Universe, or whatever Higher Power we can believe in could restore us to sanity.

We don't have to know it. We have only to believe it. If we are still having difficulty accepting that we are insane, let us look at our behavior since we thought we took the First Step. Did we really admit we were powerless and that our lives had become unmanageable? If we did, are we still trying to manage our own lives even though we know we are powerless and that our lives cannot be managed? If we are powerless and our lives are un manageable, and we continue nevertheless to try and manage our lives, what we are actually doing is continuing day after day, month in and month out, to try to do something we know is impossible. Anyone who indefinitely continues to attempt what he or she knows cannot be done is insane by any definition.

To be ready to stop attempting the impossible is a step toward sanity. And since we know we are powerless, there has to be a Power greater than our powerlessness. By associating with others who have taken the Twelve Steps we will see many examples of how their Higher Power has restored their sanity. We must conclude that our own Higher Power can do the same for us.

When we finally realize we are as insane as the society that perverted our purpose in living and come to believe there must be a Higher Power that can restore us to sanity, Step Two will take us just as Step One took us. When this happens, we will have the faith necessary to turn over a new leaf and try Step Three.

step three

Made a decision to turn our will and our lives over to the care of God *as we understood Him*.

OUR WILL IS WHAT WE THINK, our power to reason, learn, make decisions, experience. Our will is our consciousness. Our lives are the ability to breathe, touch, taste, smell and exist. Our will and our lives together are all that we are. Without them we are nothing. We don't exist.

What is suggested in the Third Step is that we turn everything we are, our very existence, over to the care of a God we probably do not understand at all. We may not even be certain a God exists, yet this Step suggests we turn our will and our lives over to that unknown and possibly nonexistent Power.

Wow!

That is something to chew on, and we may be expected to chew on it for a long time before we can bring ourselves to do it. In the first place most of us have been taught to pray to God, to petition Him for help or guidance in managing our lives. We have been taught to make a servant out of God and get Him to help us attain goals and do things we have already decided upon before we turn to God for assistance. That is a lot different than turning our very fiber and essence over to Him to do with whatever He wants without even consulting our own desires. We have been taught to pray for people, places and things, not to surrender ourselves completely to an unknown Power and gamble on what will become of us.

That's quite an order for those of us taught from birth to get down on our knees and specify exactly what we want God to do for us. We are being asked to submit ourselves to white magic. But the only experience we have had in the past is with black magic. Black magic is making use of supernatural power to help us accomplish what we have already determined to accomplish. White magic is just the opposite . . . to surrender to the Supernatural and allow It to take over, manage and direct our every activity.

Black magic, in making a servant out of God, ceases to be supernatural and becomes superhuman. Superhuman power is black magic, no matter how it is used. Practitioners of black magic usually believe they are practicing white magic. They rationalize this by saying, *I only pray for positive purposes* or *I only pray for others, never for my own profit*. Nevertheless, the unwitting black magician is still telling God what to do instead of letting God tell us what to do.

Step Three

White magic is letting God run the show. The Third Step suggests we turn our will and our lives over to the care of God, whether we understand Him or not, and let Him run our lives, with no strings attached.

At first we are apt to only turn problems over to God. And we may not be conditioned to even do that until we feel we have done everything we can to solve the problems first. "God expects us to do the footwork," we will say to one another in support of the old ideas we were programmed with long before we ever heard of the Twelve Steps to success and happiness. "God gave us the brains, talent, muscle and willpower to solve our problems, and we must exhaust these God-given resources before we may turn our problems over to Him."

And it may seem to work that way for awhile. Each problem then can be handled like a basketball in the hands of a player. After he has done everything he possibly can with the ball and is cornered by all the other players, then and only then may he pass the ball over their heads. "O.K. Buster. You take it!" he may shout and fling the ball. Even if there is no Buster somewhere down the court, the player will be rid of the ball. So we may for awhile handle our problems. We may knuckle down and do everything we can possibly do to solve our problems, and only then may we pass them along to an ephemeral God.

THE TWELVE STEPS TO HAPPINESS

Even an atheist can do this. It doesn't matter whether *Buster* is somewhere down the floor or not. Once the ballplayer has passed the ball, he no longer has the problem. It becomes Buster's problem, whether there is a Buster or not. All the player has to do to get rid of the ball is take a chance that *there may be a Buster*. But Buster or no, the ball is no longer the player's problem.

Those who have *handled* their problems this way, one problem at a time, experience one of the smaller miracles of the Twelve Steps. When they finally turn their problems over to God, even if only because they have exhausted their own abilities, the problems do seem to go away until they are either solved or not solved. The miracle is that those who attempt Step Three no longer have to worry about problems they have finally turned over to God. They let God worry over them. They begin to sleep at night. They start to wake up more relaxed each morning and feel better all the time. But they are still very near to specifying what they want God to do for them. They have not turned their whole lives over to Him, the good as well as the bad. They have only turned problems over to God.

Once God has taken over enough problems to prove even to skeptics that He exists, a peculiar thing happens. It stops working. It is almost as if the player's basketball gets more difficult to get rid of. *Here, Buster* the player yells. *You take it!* He tries to throw the ball, but it doesn't want to leave his fingers.

After awhile the player, who thinks he is practicing the Third Step by turning only one problem at a time over to God, discovers that God doesn't seem to be taking the problems any more. It is almost as if God were saying, "All right. Now that you know I am here, why don't you go ahead and take the Third Step? Turn your will and your life, everything you are, over to Me and accept whatever happens as the will of God. This business of only giving Me problems after you have done everything you can to louse them up has run its course. Get on with the Third Step. I want it all."

But that is still quite an order. Obviously, God is not another unseen basketball player somewhere down the floor. Even if He were so easily identified, would it be any easier to turn our will and our lives over to Him? "What is God?" we may ask if we are agnostic. "How can I turn my entire being and future over to some Power I don't understand and am not even sure exists?" Well nobody said it wouldn't require us to take a gamble on the Unknown. Nobody knows what or whom God is. No one understands God. Whenever you meet someone who claims to know what God is or what God wants you to do or not to do, beware. You are meeting a leader and a liar.

The Twelve Steps do not explain God or attempt

to con you into behaving the way any other human believes God wants you to behave. The Twelve Steps are not a religious program, yet they may be followed by Christians, Jews, Buddhists, Taoists, Confucianists, Moslems, Humanists, Agnostics or Atheists, providing they are willing to take a chance that all their old beliefs may not be true. The Twelve Steps are a spiritual program. Step Three is an opportunity to let a Spirit greater than our own take charge of the rest of our lives.

It is not necessary to understand a Higher Power to let It take over. It is only necessary to believe It might do so for our own well-being. If we don't believe that, we are trying to progress too fast in the program. Step Two was coming *to believe that a Power greater than ourselves could restore us to sanity*. If we don't believe that enough to take a chance on It, then we haven't done Step Two yet and must go back to it.

It is impossible to take Step Three unless we believe *a Power greater than ourselves can restore us to sanity,* which is Step Two. If we are still having trouble with Step Three, it is probably because we didn't really take Step Two.

Or is it because we are afraid God will change some of the things we enjoy about ourselves if we allow Him to take over? Perhaps we are afraid some of the religious puritans or bigots might be right in their concept of what God wants us to do and not to do. We don't want to be a puritan or a bigot, and we are afraid God might turn us into some kind of righteous snob if we leave it up to Him. As much as we have been trained to worship saints, there is something about them we don't like that makes us not want to be saints.

Confusion about sex could be keeping us from taking the Third Step. We could be afraid that God, given our permission to do with us what He will, might change our attitudes about sex. We might fear that puritanical restrictions we no longer believe about sex might be God's way after all. Maybe we like our individually acquired degrees of sexual freedom so much we are afraid God will louse up our sex lives if we let Him. That could be a big barrier to taking the Third Step. Will God destroy our sexual appetites if we turn our wills and lives over to Him?

That's something we will just have to take a chance on, isn't it? If we want the happiness and success millions of people have found by taking the Twelve Steps, *we must be willing to go to any lengths to get it*. The Twelve Steps have not yet turned anyone into a saint. *There are no saints in this program.* There are no reports of loss of sexual appetites from those who have taken Step Three. On the contrary, there are countless testimonials that sexual capacity and happiness are miraculously increased for those who have taken all Twelve Steps.

"All right," we must say. "I'll take a chance."

And it helps to do this aloud. We may look in the direction we think God might be and call out, "Take over my will and my life and do with me what You may! I give them to Your care with no strings attached!" And we may mention whatever we fear most and leave it up to Him to sort and direct our future forever, anyway He chooses. "From now on," we may call out, "anything You say goes! I am all Yours!"

Don't expect a flash of light or the earth to move. But you can at least expect a strange calm to follow your commitment. A load may seem to float off your shoulders. It can happen right away or gradually over a day or two as your consciousness begins to recognize that a Higher Power indeed seems to be taking over when you let It do so.

But we have been trained a long, long time to do everything ourselves. It will be only too easy to take our wills and lives back from the care of God unless we are resolved not to do so. A good way to guard against this is to repeat the commitment each morning, one day at a time, for perhaps a thousand good mornings. "I'm all Yours, God," you may repeat in your own words. "I will accept anything You do with me today."

It will be difficult at first not to compare what is happening to you each day with what you would have planned if you were still in charge. And from time to time you might not like the way things appear to be going. But if you remember your promise to accept whatever happens to you in God's care, you will begin to notice something wonderful. There seems to be a plan. Things which appear to be unpleasant at first always seem to lead to something good. This happens so often you begin to anticipate it. After awhile when something appears to be going wrong in a way you would never have planned, you start to wonder, "What do you suppose this is leading to?"

Turning our wills and lives over to the care of God as we understand Him does not lead to a permanent state of euphoria. But God now seems to give us everything we need. He gives us all the joy and sadness we need, the problems and solutions we need, as well as the achievements and failures we need.

We still have depressions, but they always seem to be followed by highs. We may hope for permanent serenity, which we have prayed for in the prayer of St. Francis of Assisi, but we will never have permanent serenity until we are ready to be buried. There is no such thing as a lifetime of serenity if we accept the adventures, excitements and ecstasies provided us by God.

And if for a thousand days we continue to turn our wills and our lives over to the care of God, it will become a habit. And the habit will be just as strong as the one we once had of trying to run the entire show ourselves.

You will discover beyond doubt that surrendering

your will to God has not turned you into some kind of vegetable waiting around for something to happen. In fact, you will become more active than ever. You won't have to waste time planning goals any more, and you will have more time and energy for achievement.

When you give up managing your life, friends will compliment you on how well you appear to be managing it. When you stop trying to keep yourself on a narrow track of self-discipline, people will start admiring the discipline you seem to have. Yet, if you confess to them that you do not manage your own life, no longer set goals or practice self-discipline, they will think you are joking. In fact, a better manager than you will have taken over, and you will be given credit for His management. Yet, inside you will know you are no longer responsible, need no longer blame yourself for apparent mistakes, and cannot really accept credit for the successes God directs for you.

To be a success is to do what you want to do. One day, having committed your will to the care of God, you will come to trust it and realize your wants are created by Him in your will and nowhere else. This means you can trust your will and do what it wants to. Either that, or you didn't really turn your will over to Him. It's the greatest cop-out of all time. And that's exactly what it is. A glorious cop-out. From now on, with your will in the care of God, you can trust it and do what you want to do, one day at a time for the rest of your life. That's not a bad way to live.

Now a word about a certain word. The word is decision. We find it in the first part of the Third Step. *Made a decision* to turn our will and our lives over to the care of God as we understood Him.

There are those who will rationalize that this means we do not actually have to turn our wills and lives over to God at this point. All we have to do is make a decision to do so. Then we can put off executing the decision until some later date. This, of course, is rubbish. It is an instinct conditioned by our former way of life in which we set goals and tried to manage our lives to achieve them.

If we think we are making a decision to do something, not now but later, what we are really doing is making a decision to postpone doing it. It becomes a decision not to do something. That is not the decision called for in the Third Step.

The Third Step is to decide to do it. When we decide to do something we do it, not postpone it. So when you decide to turn your will and your life over to the care of God, that is precisely what you will do. The only proof that you have decided to do this, rather than to procrastinate, is that you do it. Decision leads to action. Are you ready for it? Go ahead if you are. Ask God to take care of your will and your life. Ask whatever God you understand or don't understand. Take the big gamble.

Have you turned your will and your life over to the care of God as you understand Him? If you have, you are ready to work on Step Four.

step four

Made a searching and fearless moral inventory of ourselves.

H*ERE IS A STEP WHICH AT FIRST*
and last may appear to be fun. We are asked to
examine our own lives. What to the average person
could be more fascinating than that?

Our first instinct, one which may persist for a
long time, is to look back and try to experience
total recall about all the naughty or dastardly things
we did in our pasts. Most of these moments of
recall will be very entertaining. Many things we
did, despite our upbringing not to do them, were
fun. But, here and there in recalling the past, we
will find things we are ashamed of, misdeeds that
still make us feel guilty. And digging up skeletons
we hid in our own closets can resurrect painful
shame and remorse. There may be incidents in our
past that make us disgusted with ourselves to the
point of self-repulsion. Some of these unsavory episodes in our well-hidden histories might be awful
enough to make us afraid to resurrect them.

So it may be that digging through our hidden

closets will not turn out to be as much fun as we first thought. It is not entertaining to make ourselves feel guilty. We often will procrastinate and resist bringing fresh light to dark episodes. Fear of what else we will find in our secret recesses might make us afraid to go on with the Fourth Step. We could rationalize that it would be better to move on to Step Five and *admit to God and to another person the exact nature of our wrongs*.

But how can we admit to another what we can't admit to ourselves? Like it or not, we appear to be stuck with taking Step Four before we can go on with the Twelve Steps.

Then why is it so difficult to make a *searching and fearless* moral inventory? Perhaps a dictionary can tell us why this Step is so hard to complete. The *American Heritage Dictionary* defines *fearless* as being *without a feeling of alarm or disquiet caused by awareness or expectation of danger, or without being afraid of something*. Isn't that odd? We probably thought to take a *fearless* moral inventory of ourselves meant to bravely research our past and courageously recount the history of our misdeeds. Yet in no dictionary on earth does the word *fearless* mean to be brave. It means *without fear*. Without fear there is no need to be brave.

Then how can we dig through the past we are afraid of, resurrect guilts that frighten us and be without fear? The answer is we can't. As long as our inventory contains anything we are afraid of we can't take a *fearless inventory* which means an *inventory without fear in it*. That definition bears repeating. *Fearless* means *without fear*. An inventory that makes us afraid is not fearless. It is an inventory with fear. We can bravely take all the frightening inventories we wish, but none of them will be a *fearless* moral inventory.

What is there about our inventory that arouses fear? There may be something in our past which makes us feel guilty, probably because we are guilty, and we are, therefore, afraid to face our guilt. What we are actually afraid of is that whatever made us commit those guilty acts in the past may make us commit equally guilty acts in the future. There is a step ahead among the Twelve Steps that will enable us to eliminate the only valid guilt that may remain from past misdeeds.

The important thing for us to learn in taking this Fourth Step is that the past no longer exists. Only the present exists, which means the future does not yet exist either.

Perhaps we ought to turn to the dictionary again. Let us look up the word *inventory* and see if understanding the true meaning of that word can help us take an inventory without fear in it. According to the *American Heritage Dictionary*, an inventory is a *detailed list of things, especially a periodic survey of goods and materials in stock*. The same dictionary says a history is *a narrative of events or a chronological record of events*.

In digging up unsavory misdeeds of our past are

we taking an inventory or a history? Nowhere in the definition of inventory is any mention made of a history, nor in the meaning of history is the word inventory used. Obviously *an inventory is not a history*. A store when taking an inventory does not count what used to be sold there, but only what is currently in stock. Perhaps if we take an inventory of ourselves instead of a history, we will find nothing to be afraid of. Then, and only then, can it be a *fearless inventory*.

Obviously, instead of looking into our past for things no longer included in our inventory, we must instead look to see what is there right now. We must count what is in stock at this very instant, not what was there in the past. What do we find in our inventory? Qualities to look for are pride and false pride, generosity and selfishness, compassion and self-pity, hate and love, anger and peace, worry and sloth, kindness and meanness, and all other positives and negatives we can pinpoint in our own present lives.

We must look at the good as well as the bad. Were we to count only the evil in ourselves, we would be taking an immoral inventory rather than a moral one. The Fourth Step gives us a chance to stand back and look at our pluses as well as our minuses. Each of us has different standards about what is good and bad. The same qualities one person may put on the minus side in his inventory may appear on the plus side in another's.

To be thorough, the inventory should be written on paper. The mind is like the memory bank of a computer. The act of taking pen in hand and starting to write turns the computer on. What comes out on paper may amaze you. You will discover great truths, both pleasing and frightening, that you never thought you knew about yourself. But if anything frightening remains there, you are merely taking an inventory. And if there is fear in it, you cannot succeed in completing the Fourth Step.

Then how do we get the fear out of our inventory? We are like the buyer in a store who is afraid he did not stock his department properly. Therefore he fears the inventory, for it will show him up as incapable of fulfilling his responsibility to the store. But what if the buyer lets a higher boss select the goods to fill his department? Then what the inventory turns up is no longer the buyer's responsibility. It is the responsibility of the buyer's boss. The buyer cannot be blamed, nor can he blame himself for what the boss put in the inventory. The buyer has nothing to fear.

So, if we are to take a searching and *fearless* moral inventory of ourselves, we had better let someone else stock the store. That someone is God, may you find Him now. And if you haven't, it simply means you did not really take the previous Step. In the Third Step you were supposed to turn your will and your life, which is everything you are, over to God. If you are still afraid, you did not do so. Do it now. Turn your will over to the care of God, even if you don't understand Him. Take a chance. Gamble that your will is in the complete care of a Higher Power now responsible for everything, every thought and desire in your will. If you can assume your will is in the care of God, you should be able to trust it. At least you can gamble on it and take a chance that you are no longer responsible for your inventory. If you can't take that chance, you did not really do the previous Step.

So go ahead. Once and for all, turn your will along with your life over to God's care, whether you understand Him or not. Once you have done that, there will be nothing to fear in your will and you can proceed to take a fearless inventory. You have a right to assume, once you have turned your will over, that whatever you find in it has been put there by God. You need not take blame nor credit for anything God places there. We are back to the great cop-out. And that is just where we have to be in order to take an inventory with nothing to fear in it.

The Fourth Step is actually the first of several tests by which you can determine whether you have completed the Third Step. If you have completed Steps Three and Four, no courage will be required to proceed. The simple directions on the next page will tell you how to move ahead and take Step Five. No courage will be needed, because your inventory no longer contains fear. And without fear, what need is there to be brave?

You can tell by the way you feel that you are progressing nicely toward the success and happiness that come slowly, but surely, with completion of all Twelve Steps. So, let's move on.

step five

Admitted to God, to ourselves, and to another human being, the exact nature of our wrongs.

HERE IS A UNIQUE OPPORTUNITY, perhaps for the first time in our lives, to become honest.

First, we have to admit our wrongs to God. That shouldn't be difficult. After all God isn't likely to tell anyone, because God hasn't appeared to be gossiping lately with anyone we know. So admitting our wrongs to God appears to be the only way we can confide without the fear that confidential disclosures will be betrayed to fellow men and women. But how do we go about admitting something to God?

We simply confess to Him. Catholics have been doing this for centuries by stepping into concealing booths and reciting sins to a priest who listens on behalf of God. This ought to be easy for Catholics to do. However, those of other religions, or of no particular religion at all, will have to enumerate the wrongs directly to their Higher Power as they understand Him, or even if they do not understand

Him. This direct talk to God can be done the same way that we turned our wills and lives over to the care of God in the Third Step. Both these contacts are direct. In the Third Step, we give ourselves to God. In the Fifth Step, we tell something to God. We tell Him what our wrongs are. Not what they were before we took a fearless inventory, but what wrongs we still find in our make-ups today, even after we think we have turned our wills and our lives over to God's care.

Perhaps we still worry. That is a wrong we must tell God about, for worrying means we do not trust in the future God is about to give us.

Perhaps we are still setting goals and struggling to achieve them. We must admit that to God, because setting goals, even if we pray for God to help us achieve them, means we are still trying to manage our lives instead of letting Him do so. Instead of letting God be our manager, we are praying for Him to be our servant.

Maybe we resent or hate someone or something. We've got to admit it to God, because hating or resenting means we do not accept the offending person or thing as part of God's plan for us.

If we have listed self-pity in the previous Step's inventory, we now can tell God our wrong is that we are dissatisfied with the position or condition God has placed us in today.

It could be we find ourselves jealous or possessive. We must admit these wrongs to God because jealousy and possessiveness indicate a desire to control or dominate others. And how can we manage others when we cannot manage ourselves? We cannot have truly turned our wills and our lives over to the care of God without accepting the behavior of others exactly as God presents them to us.

In each case we will address our Higher Power about traits in ourselves that give us discomfort, guilt or unhappiness. By doing so we will discover that the *nature* of these wrongs is that they are feelings or motivations we ourselves feel responsible for when we should have turned all responsibility over to God.

In no case will the nature of a wrong be a misdeed, although the nature may be that which causes us to perform a misdeed. What we are looking for here are motives, not actions. We are looking into our very natures to learn why we continue to try to alter God's intentions for us. We admit to Him we are still trying to run the show instead of letting Him run it.

Once we have admitted to God the exact nature of these wrongs, we must find another human being we trust enough to confide these weaknesses to. At this point, though it is obvious that a recitation of past sins is not called for, we may exert utmost caution in selecting a confidant. It is as if total confession of prior evil acts is about to lay us bare and vulnerable to another human being.

We may even decide to admit our wrongs piecemeal to various persons. This is so we can find others guilty of what we think might be certain infractions of God's laws. That way we will not have to confess particular offenses to anyone who is not as guilty of the same misdeeds as we are. Very often the differences between our feelings about sex and what we have been taught is proper may drive us to these extremes. Thieves will seek thieves to confide in. Murderers will confess only to other murderers.

The point is that we are not admitting to God, to ourselves and to another human being that we have lied, stolen or murdered. What we are doing is admitting to God, to ourselves and to somebody else what we are like now, and what about ourselves is currently wrong. Not what used to be wrong.

But why is there anything wrong now that we have turned our wills and our lives over to the care of God? Perhaps the nature of our wrong is that we did not let go of our wills, and our wills therefore have not let go of our lives.

We must ask ourselves, "Do we trust our wills?" If my will urges me to go ahead and do something that prior conditioning by society tells me not to do, which do I trust? The will I have turned over to the care of God or the will previously conditioned by society? If I have turned my will over to God, I will trust it. Either that, or I did not turn it over. If I let society overrule my will, which is in

God's care, I am exerting self-management and not allowing God-management to occur.

My Creator must be permitted to create what society seeks to control—my desires. If my will, which is all the consciousness I possess, is in God's care, then God alone will create the desires He puts into my will. If I lack courage to go ahead and do the things God makes my will want to do, then the nature of my wrong is that I trust society more than I trust God. I lack the courage needed to gamble that my wants are now being created by God. I am afraid God may not actually be taking care of my will and creating my wants.

This is understandable, because many things I want to do are things society taught me were wrong before I ever heard of the Twelve Steps. This may make me doubt God actually has taken over my will, even though I asked Him to.

The nature of my wrong might be lack of faith.

It could be lack of courage.

It could be fear. Fear to go ahead and do what I want to in the face of prior training by society. If there is fear, it means we have not taken the Step before this one. We have not yet taken a fearless inventory. And we have not taken the Third Step. If we have not turned our wills and lives over to the care of God, now is the time to do so. Then we can go ahead with Step Four, return to where we are now and again admit to God, to ourselves and to another human being the exact nature of our wrongs.

When we have shared our weaknesses three ways; with someone else, ourselves, and with God, we may move ahead to the next Step.

step six

Were entirely ready to have God remove all these defects of character.

THE VERY PROSPECT OF HAVING all defects of character removed may seem undesirable to anyone who has not yet completed the five Steps that led to this one. What kind of defects are we talking about? Are we referring to our inclination to steal, or commit violence, or to double park or write bad checks? Well, we could be referring to the defects of character which cause us to do these things, if we still do them. But if that's all there is to it, being ready to have such defects removed would be easy.

However, we might admit there may be defects of character we enjoy so much we are not ready to have God or anyone else, including ourselves, remove them. Are we talking about overeating, overdrinking, smoking too much or taking drugs? Not likely. If we are still doing things like that, we are probably not this far along in the program. If we have turned our wills and lives over to the care of God, He is not likely to continue indefinitely to create the kinds of compulsive wants in us that are damaging to the bodies He placed us in. Besides, which of us would not be willing to have God remove our compulsions to overdrink, overeat, oversmoke, or misuse drugs? How could we not wish God to remove defects of character that would make us continue those kinds of insane practices?

Perhaps we are still on a power trip. We may enjoy trying to manage our own lives and as many other lives as we can so much that we don't want to give God a chance to remove this defect of character. For if we have admitted our own lives are unmanageable, then how can we manage other people's lives? To continue to try to do so must certainly be a defect of character. To give up even the illusion of power may be more than we are willing to do. Yet give it up we must if we are ready to have God remove all our defects of character.

Or perhaps we think the task of removing all our character defects is more than we can handle. Well, we are right. It is more than we can handle by ourselves. And to delay taking this Step because we are afraid of the overwhelming job of trying to remove our own character defects simply means we do not yet understand the simple words used in the Step. Step Six does not say we are ready *to remove* all these defects of character. It says we are ready *to have God remove* them.

There is a difference. All of us have been taught

since birth to try to improve ourselves, strengthen our own characters and make ourselves good moral citizens. To stop trying to remove our own character defects and become ready to let God take over that task may be extremely difficult for us. After all, our parents, teachers, preachers, employers, psychologists and most philosophers have been telling us all our lives that our duty to them and to God is to work on our own defects, improve them and try to eliminate them. This impossible responsibility has been so drummed into us that the idea of relinquishing it to God seems almost sacrilegious.

"Well," someone will inevitably reason, "God may remove our defects, but He expects us to do the footwork. We can't just sit around and be vegetables and expect Him to do all the work. God expects us to work on our defects. He gave us brains and expects us to use them." This kind of false logic can be used to procrastinate taking the Sixth Step indefinitely. The fact is, that if you allow God to take over your will and your life and become ready to have Him remove all your defects of character, you are in no way preparing to become a vegetable. Allowing God to control your mind and being willing to have Him improve your character would only lead to inaction if God wished you to be inactive. And why would your Creator who gave you both mind and body wish you not to use them? The trick is, are you going to make a commitment to let God direct your use of mind and body, or are you going to continue to be in charge the way an obviously troubled society taught you to be before you ever heard of these Twelve Steps?

Which is it to be? You? Or God? Who are you ready to let remove all your defects of character? This is the Step that clarifies the difference between the Creator and the created. Only humankind can make defects. Only God can remove them. Yet, we are still reluctant to let Him do so. Why? Because we are afraid He might remove something from our characters that we enjoy.

What are we talking about? Cheating at cards? Perhaps, if we still insist on winning games enough to withhold our very souls from God's control. But this is no more likely than that our procrastination is based on love of violence, or dishonesty, or power. If it is any of these things, we must accept the evidence that we still have not irrevocably taken Step Three which was to turn our wills and lives over to the care of God. For God would not have us procrastinating this way at all. In God's hands our wills will want to go ahead and take all Twelve Steps to success and happiness.

Step Six, like Steps Four and Five before it, is a test to see if we have really taken Step Three. If we have not, then what is still holding us up? What are the potential defects we enjoy so much we don't wish to give them up?

Society has taught us so many restrictions that we don't know what is right and what is wrong. Many things that society has preached or legislated against are practices we may still have an appetite for. We don't want to take a chance that certain taboos dictated by one segment or another of society might be restrictions God would have us observe if we completely give up to His management.

The fact is, most of us are so confused by sociological attitudes that we don't wish to gamble on the possibility some of our own appetites, practices or fantasies might be defects of character. Being ready to have God remove our character defects might lay ourselves open to having some of our present wants reduced or removed. And to have them redirected, reduced or eliminated is not compatible with anything we hope for. If becoming happy and successful means cutting back either in practice or in dreams, who wants success or happiness?

Well, have no fear. The Twelve Steps are not a religious program, nor a program of morality. Morality is the imposition of one person's or group's code of conduct on another person or group, no more or no less than that. The principles of the Twelve Steps have nothing to do with morality. They may be applied to a religion or moral code and enhance it. But it will not work the other way around. To apply a moral code or religion to these Steps can only change their principles. The Steps are not open to moral, religious or any other kind of interpretation. Those who interpret the Steps fail to find success and happiness. Those who simply read and do what they say, succeed and are happy. It is that simple.

Fundamental drives do not diminish in the hands of God. The only way to prove this to your own satisfaction is to gamble on it. The ultimate gamble it to become ready to have God remove all your defects of character and then wait to see what He removes.

In the final analysis do you really know what your defects of character are? Have you not, in taking the Steps leading to this one, changed your mind about what your strengths and weaknesses are; what is good and what is bad? Have you not learned that society, and you through society, have been wrong about many things? And that only by discovering you were wrong have you learned the truth?

Then rest assured that in God's hands only that which is not natural about your instincts can be removed when you are ready to let Him get rid of your defects. What is natural will grow stronger. The only way you can get maximum enjoyment out of your wants is with certain knowledge that your wants are created by God, no matter what any other person or group believes.

Belief is a substitute for knowledge. The way to learn what God has in mind for you, sexually, materially or any other way is to be ready to have Him remove your desire for everything He does not wish you to do. You've got to take that big gamble again in a more defined area of your life and say something like, "O.K. I'm ready to have You remove all my defects of character whether You take away something I like or not."

At least three million people have taken this Step and remained vibrantly alive. You may also believe that whatever joyous activities God alone may make you want to engage in, you will be able to do better than you have ever done before. Being ready for God to remove our defects is being ready for Him to erase our guilt about all the wonderful things He makes us want to do. Without guilt we are free.

But Step Six is not an action Step that we actually take. It is a state of being that takes us. One day we suddenly realize we no longer have any qualms about letting God remove any and all of our character defects as He sees fit. It is not that we figure once God removes our favorite defects we won't miss them. It is that we come to believe, judging by what others who took these Steps told us, that we can trust God. Our Higher Power will get us into better shape to enjoy pleasure than we have ever been before. And He will provide us with more pleasures than we have ever dreamed of. All we have to do is leave it up to Him. It is only when we are ready to receive so much joy that we discover we are ready to have God remove whatever defects of character He wants to.

How do we know when we have finally completed this Step? We can tell by moving to Step Seven. The proof that we have accepted Step Six is our willingness to go ahead with the Seventh Step.

So, take a look at the next page. Are you willing to commit yourself to God's action enough to ask Him to do what you think you are ready to have happen? If you are, you have taken the Sixth Step. If you are not, stick with the Sixth Step until you can believe it.

If you are willing to let God remove your character defects, go on to Step Seven.

step seven

**Humbly asked Him to
remove our shortcomings.**

NOW IS THE TIME FOR ACTION
again. The time has come to fish or cut bait. Here
is where you go ahead and ask for what you claim
to be ready to have happen; where you humbly ask
God to remove your shortcomings.

Many of us will take out our inventory again,
prepare to go through our list of character defects
and apply the principle of living one day at a time
to them. In other words it may seem logical to us
to select and tackle only one defect at a time. We
may ask for God's guidance in licking jealousy, for
instance. And we may set about working on this
problem of ours, which is obviously a shortcoming, and pray to God for help in successfully wip-
ing jealousy out of our lives.

Then we may move on to lust, which we have
been taught is a character defect, and ask God's
help in eliminating that problem from our lives.
Next we could go on to anger, or resentment, or
self-pity and seek God's assistance in the difficult

tasks we now face in removing these shortcomings from our inventory.

No one is perfect, we may reason. Therefore, we will never really hope to eliminate all our character defects no matter how hard we work at it and no matter how much we pray for guidance.

"There are no saints in this program," many a struggling old timer will quote. "We just do the best we can." And being familiar with the language, if not the philosophy, we may subconsciously complete that sentence. We just do the best we can *to do what*? Why *to become saints*, of course.

And that means we must learn to live by the rules quoted in books the other saints ahead of us lived, died and were sainted for trying to obey. It means we must try at the very least to eliminate from our behavior those things forbidden by our religion and our society.

But wait a minute! Let us remember again that this is not a religious program. Let us again acknowledge that *the principles of these Steps are diametrically opposite to everything society has heretofore taught us*.

The reason there are no saints in this program is that these Steps make no suggestion that we attempt to become saints. Or that we, by our own efforts, attempt to fit any image at all. What Step Seven suggests is that we humbly ask *Him* to remove our shortcomings. Not *us*. *Him*.

"Hey wait a minute," we may again argue. "God surely doesn't expect me to lie around and wait for Him to do all the work. Surely, He expects me to put forth some effort."

Well, that certainly fits the hard-work-and-do-it-yourself ethic we have been taught all our lives. But let us not try to change the meaning of Step Seven to make it fit what we already believe. Let us get rid of our old ideas about what is right and wrong long enough to read what the Step actually says. It says, *Humbly asked Him to remove our shortcomings.*

You don't hand your car key to someone, humbly ask that person to park your car, then grab the key back and do it yourself. That wouldn't be humbly asking anyone to do anything. It would be arrogantly demonstrating you feel more competent to park it yourself than the person you asked. You don't humbly ask God to remove your shortcomings and then, instead of allowing Him to remove them, insist upon removing them yourself. It would not be humbly asking God to do something unless you let Him do so. Even to ask God for guidance so you can do it yourself is not the same as asking Him to remove your shortcomings and humbly accepting what follows as His intent, not yours.

This Step can only be taken sincerely. We are not taking the Step at all if we mouth a request for God to remove our defects with no intention of letting Him do so, because we would rather do it

ourselves, with God's help perhaps, but still cling-
ing to responsibility for the success or failure of
the task. Not many human beings throughout history have been credited with removing all their defects of character. So if we try to remove them all,
we are doomed to failure. But if we give up trying
to remove all our shortcomings and humbly ask
God to do so, it becomes His responsibility, not
ours. There is no way we can accept either credit
or blame for what follows. Therefore we cannot
fail. Only God can fail, and He cannot.

What remains in our inventory after we have
humbly asked God to remove our shortcomings
must belong there. Some remaining characteristics
may be things we used to think were defects, but
since God has left them in us, we can assume God
put them there for His purpose and does not intend
to remove them. Therefore, we will learn that not
all things we suspected were shortcomings are defects after all. Some of our suspected weaknesses
will turn out to be strengths, perhaps not in our
neighbors' eyes, but in the sight of God who leaves
them now in the souls He created.

Those whom He wishes to be leaders will be left
with a desire for power, but no wish to misuse it.
Those He wishes to be lovers will be left with ex-
quisite sexuality, but with enough consideration not
to hurt anyone with it. Those He wants to be materially wealthy will be, but without the greed and
possessiveness that cause wealth to be a burden to

others. God will not remove pain from our lives, because if we cannot feel when we are pinched, we will not feel when we are kissed. The greatest defect God, if we let Him, will remove from our lives is the shortcoming of egotism. In our hearts we will be unable to take credit for the improvements in our lives. We will give credit where it is due, to God whom we trusted to take away our shortcomings no matter what they might turn out to be. And for the first time in our lives, we will be certain what our weaknesses were and what our strengths are. The weaknesses will be what God removes from our lives. The strengths will be what He permits to stay. And this will remain true only as long as we allow Him to be fully in charge.

Instead of being responsible, we will have become respondable. Having asked Him to remove our shortcomings, we may assume the way we feel about what He presents to us throughout His daily gift of life is the way He makes us feel. And so we may do what we feel like doing about whatever comes along. It is a reaffirmation of the Third Step. Our lives are in God's care, so what happens to us is His plan. Our wills are in His care, so we can trust our wills to tell us what to do. We asked God to remove our shortcomings and humbly trust Him to do His will with them, so we need not fear our weaknesses any more.

Do we find ourselves sitting back and letting God do everything? No. We do find that God gives us plenty to do and makes us want to do more than ever. And we need no longer waste time trying to decide what we should do or should not do. Now we try to go ahead and do everything He makes us want to do, and nothing He makes us not want to do. We learn, timidly at first, to trust the intuitions He gives us rather than continue the mistrust of intuition pounded into us by an insecure society. The reason we remain timid about this is because it is not easy to overcome long established habits. Our churches, employers and government have had us obediently consulting them for years about everything we should or should not do. Dependence upon an insane society's rules and regulations is a long-standing habit difficult to break. So we must form a new habit.

Just as for however many days it took, one day at a time, we began each morning by asking God to take care of our wills and our lives until it became a habit to let Him do so, we must now do the same with this Step. Each day we must humbly ask Him to remove our shortcomings until it has become a daily routine to let Him do so. Only then will we have broken the bonds of our old ideas of correct and incorrect behavior. Then, and not before, we will begin to trust our feelings as being our only conscious contact with God who creates the way we feel. We will come to know that the feelings God alone gives us are His instructions. We may obey them without fear.

But if we are afraid to obey the feelings God gives us, then fear is still in our inventory, and we have not yet completed *Step Four*. With fear still in our hearts we have not yet taken the *fearless* moral inventory. The reason we have not done so remains the same. We have not yet, in spite of all our efforts, fully *turned our wills and our lives over to the care of God as we understand Him*. The Seventh Step, like Steps Four, Five and Six before it, will keep bouncing back to Step Three until we finally get around to doing what those simple words suggest.

Did you think it was going to be easy? Or that you could take these Steps quickly? Well you cannot. If you think it must be accomplished in a hurry, then impatience is one of your defects of character. And the impatience will remain until you learn to painstakingly take Steps One through Seven, no matter how long it takes or how impossible it may at times seem. When One through Six are completed, you may humbly ask God to remove your shortcomings, and your impatience will be lifted from you.

When you have become humble enough to allow God to do this in His own sweet time, you will be ready to turn the page and forge ahead to the Eighth Step toward success and happiness. Having progressed this far, you will already be happier and more successful than you have ever been before. But if you think that is something, wait and see the joyful life that awaits you when you have patiently, one step at a time, taken all Twelve Steps. However, you can't do that yet. Perhaps you are ready to take Step Eight.

step eight

Made a list of all persons we had harmed and became willing to make amends to them all.

H*ERE IS OUR CHANCE TO MAKE A* history in writing of at least part of our past lives. This is our opportunity to thoughtfully write down each of our past misdeeds and list the names of whom they had harmed. Remember the mistake many of us made in thinking Step Four, making a searching and fearless moral inventory of ourselves, meant taking count of our past sins? But then we learned an inventory is not a history. And inventory is what is in our lives now. Not what used to be there.

Well four steps later at *Step Eight*, we finally get to recount the wrongs we did to others during our troubled pasts and to honestly list by name those we have harmed. We get to face in black and white the most troublesome parts of our history, those things we are guilty of that actually caused harm to others.

We must write down their names. This is the only Step which in its language clearly specifies that we write something down, although we probably found it helpful to put the earlier inventory on paper. Whom have we harmed and how did we harm them?

Did we steal from anyone so that person suffered loss?

Did we physically injure someone?

Did we defame anyone to deliberately cause damage?

Did we lie to anyone so the lie caused harm?

Did we cheat to someone else's emotional or material disadvantage?

Did we deliberately withhold information or help from someone who suffered because we did not give it?

Did we injure someone through carelessness?

Did our laziness cause misfortune to anybody?

Did our lack of consideration for others ever result in their unhappiness or loss?

Did our greed ever deprive others of something they deserved to enjoy?

Have we maliciously meddled in the affairs of others to bring them sorrow and pain?

Have we used anyone to our own advantage but to that person's misfortune?

Have we ever committed rape?

Have we deprived anyone of a loved one by murder or by manslaughter?

Are we guilty of transmitting a disease when we knew we were infected?

Have we failed to take the responsibility we should have for a pregnancy?

Did we fail to provide for dependents in order to gratify our own desires?

Did we ever let someone be harmed when we could have prevented it?

Has our prior behavior caused anyone else mental, emotional, material or spiritual damage?

Have we let someone suffer loneliness when we should have cared?

Have we failed to give our children the educational and parental advantages they deserved?

Did we ever force our own particular moral code on someone else to that person's detriment?

Have we denied anyone equal rights because of race, creed, religion or sex?

Did we ever play a downright dirty trick on someone?

Did we ever sell anything to someone we knew could not afford it?

Have we made someone's life miserable because of our possessiveness or jealousy?

Have we ever betrayed anyone's confidence?

Have we denied our elderly who depended upon us for love and support?

Did we ever discriminate against anyone because of age?

Did we abandon anyone in distress when we should have helped?

Have we taken advantage of a position of power

to abuse anyone under our control in order to profit for ourselves?

Have we physically abused anyone?

Have we sexually abused anyone?

Did we ever let someone else take the blame and punishment for something we did?

Do we remember harming anyone at any time for any reason in any other way?

There are more ways to hurt people than these. Each of us must search our memories to identify these transgressions against others, add their names to our lists, and how we harmed them. The lists will include those we justifiably harmed. The Step says to list *all* persons we have harmed, whether we think they had it coming to them or not.

Some will find they harmed many people. Their lists will be long. Some may have actually harmed only one or two persons, so there will only be one or two names on their lists. And it is possible not to have harmed anyone except oneself. In such a case the list will be blank. Some of these will have an added difficulty in moving on to the next Step. The people who actually harmed no one in the past may not believe this could be true. Often these people will accuse themselves of not being honest in this regard.

"I've hurt people," this one may say. "I must have. I'm just not honest enough yet to admit it." And that person may be right. More soul searching never hurt anyone. It may or may not recall some actual harm done to others in the past. The important thing is that it is not a requirement that we harmed anyone. The only requirement to this Step is that if we harmed anyone we must now acknowledge that person by name and be willing to make direct amends.

We must be willing to pay whatever it may cost to make things right. We've got to be ready to accept whatever kind of embarrassment will follow if we face those we harmed, own up to what we did and take whatever measures necessary to make restitution. We will have to want to set the record straight and balance the books of our past misdeeds.

This is not yet the place to eliminate from our list those harms which restitution might damage, or those impossible to make. At this time we must be willing to make amends to *all* persons we have harmed whether it would be practical or not.

When we find we want to make things right more than we want to leave them as they are, we will have taken Step Eight and be ready to move on to Step Nine.

step nine

Made direct amends to such people wherever possible, except when to do so would injure them or others.

H*ERE'S ANOTHER ACTION STEP* that will prove whether or not we have completed the preceding Steps. If, indeed, we are willing to make amends to those we have injured, nothing will now stop us from doing so.

Step Nine will require courage. It follows that we must look up each and every individual we have damaged, contact them all and do or pay whatever is necessary to make up for what we did to them. It may mean returning to the scenes of our crimes. It will entail making direct contact with our victims. We will have to admit to their faces that we were wrong. We will have to tell them we are sorry for what we did. We must then take some kind of positive action to undo the harm we caused. However, we must take all measures to insure that in taking Step Nine we do not cause any further harm to our victims or to anyone else.

If we had an affair with someone, our past moral training might cause this to rest uneasily on our conscience. We might think the Ninth Step now gives us a chance to get it off our consciences by confessing to our former lover's mate whom we feel we wronged. But if that person didn't already know about the indiscretion of a loved one, telling about it now could only cause new pain. It could break up a relationship for no other reason that to get us off the hook. This would be a case where honesty would not pay in any currency, except grief to others. It would be a clear-cut case of trying to make amends *when to do so would injure them or others*. Confessing to someone else's guilt as well as our own would clearly cause someone else harm, so we must confess to nothing that would harm an accomplice.

If we stole from someone, we must now offer to repay what we stole.

If we physically injured anyone we must now offer to pay any medical bills we caused and compensate our victims for any other loss suffered because of the injury.

If we harmed someone by lying, we must now try to reverse the harm by telling the truth unless to do so would cause more damage by reopening old wounds.

We must confess to those we cheated and offer to repay what we defrauded them of.

Anyone who suffered because we deliberately withheld information or help should now be contacted with an offer to help in any way possible.

If we injured someone through carelessness, now is the time to offer to pay compensation for those injuries in cash or any other way we can do it.

If our laziness caused harm to someone, our hard work now must make up for it in any labor that will compensate our victim.

We will not make up for past lack of consideration by becoming considerate to those we harmed.

We must demonstrate generosity equal to the greed we displayed toward anyone we deprived.

We must apologize for maliciously meddling in the affairs of others whom we caused sorrow or pain unless to do so would cause more damage. We must offer to set the record straight or do anything we can to replace the harm with joy.

We should place ourselves at the disposal of those we used, to be used by them in any way that will make up for the misfortune we caused.

We have to offer any kind of amends that might possibly be acceptable to anyone we raped, or to the loved ones of those we deprived them of by murder or manslaughter.

We must offer any kind of reasonable settlement to anyone irresponsibly infected by us when we knew we were diseased.

It is time to sincerely offer to assume full responsibility for any pregnancy we caused, including restitution to the woman involved, and support of any resulting offspring. But not if such measures would endanger the woman's present relationship with someone else.

We must make up for any deprivation we caused our dependents in order to gratify our own desires.

We now have to take whatever measures are necessary, including full confession if it will help, to absolve anyone we allowed to take blame and punishment for something we did. We must offer to compensate in any way we can for the punishment we allowed someone else to suffer in our place.

If we let someone be harmed when we could have prevented it, we must now do something out of the ordinary to improve that person's life.

For those we have caused mental, emotional, material or spiritual damage we must now somehow contribute to their peace of mind, happiness, prosperity or spiritual well-being.

We must give companionship and attention to those we carelessly made lonely.

We must offer to provide education, as late as it may seem, to our children if we deprived them of it, and do our best to provide the security we denied them in the past.

We must apologize to anyone upon whom we forced our own moral code to their detriment, and stop trying to manage anyone else's lives.

Our bigotry must cease at once. We must compensate anyone we have deprived of equal rights because of race, creed, age, religion or sex.

We must do something equally nice for anyone we played a downright dirty trick on.

If we ever sold something to someone we knew could not afford it, we must now offer to buy it back.

Where we have made loved ones miserable by possessiveness or jealousy, we should now give them the gift of privacy and freedom.

We must do whatever we can think of to bring peace of mind and body to anyone we have physically or mentally abused.

We must offer our regrets to anybody whose confidence we betrayed and agree to make up for it in some positive way.

Those under our power whom we have abused for our own profit or advancement must now be given our love and assistance.

There are many ways to attempt to undo the harm we have done to others. We must honestly and directly set about offsetting the damage we have done to every person we have abused. A great deal of this Step can be accomplished by learning to love those we hated and to pray for those we cursed.

In repairing the damage we did to others, we will most certainly be overhauling our own lives. If we do this job thoroughly enough, we can find ourselves returned to an amazing pure state without hatred, guilt or resentment. It will probably be the first time we have experienced this freedom from negative emotions since society began to distort us from the natural creations that appeared from our mother's wombs. We will feel a glow of satisfaction in knowing we have honestly done everything we can to pay off every emotional, spiritual and material debt we owe to our fellow human beings.

The importance of Step Nine is obvious. It finally gives us the chance to eradicate past concerns and start living in the present. It removes weights from our wings so we can surge up and away. We have taken this opportunity to balance evil with good, restitution will always make us feel far better than any person to whom we may offer such amends.

As difficult as it may have been to make ourselves seek out those we have harmed and replace the misery we caused with happiness, the joy we try to give will not measure up to the pleasure this Step gives us. The warm feeling of well-being resulting from taking Step Nine will make us begin to believe that indeed our wills and lives are in God's care. But belief is not enough. Remember belief is theory, and knowledge is fact.

To increase our knowledge of God's care we must now move ahead to Step Ten.

step ten

Continued to take personal inventory and when we were wrong promptly admitted it.

Remember, then, Inventory is not a history. It was not a history in the Fourth Step, and it is not a history in Step Ten. An inventory is what is in stock right now, not what used to be in stock. Merchandise sold during a pre-inventory sale is no longer in the inventory when the sale is over. A personal inventory is what is in our lives right now.

An inventory changes from day to day. Therefore to know ourselves we must continue to take personal inventories as long as we live, one day at a time.

Has greed crept back into our inventory? If so, we must admit not only that we are wrong, but how are we wrong?

Have we become dishonest? If so we must not only admit it, but also confess to ourselves why we are dishonest.

Have we become egotistical? If false pride has

returned to our inventory, we must admit it and what went wrong.

Are we back into self-pity? If so, what have we done wrong that caused this devastating defect to reenter our inventory?

How about resentment? If there is resentment in our inventory, we must admit to ourselves why we are resentful.

Are we jealous? If jealousy has come back into our inventory, we are somehow living contrary to the principles of these Steps. That is our wrong. We must find out what it is and admit it to ourselves.

Is our inventory filled with envy? Envy is a shortcoming we must not only admit to, but we must also identify and acknowledge what violation of the Twelve Step standards we are guilty of.

Do we worry again as we used to before we took the first Nine Steps? If so, we must have done one of the Steps wrong. Now is the time to admit it.

Does our inventory contain anger? It should not, unless we have done something contrary to the Twelve Step principles. We must look beyond the external situation that we are angry about. We must search within ourselves to find and admit what we are doing wrong that allows us to become angry.

Are we depressed? Let us not concern ourselves with what outside influence depresses us. Let us instead admit what wrong of our own doing permits us to feel that way.

Is the bad apple, hatred, spreading its rot throughout our inventory basket? If so, why are we, who thought we had turned our wills and our lives over to the care of God, experiencing hatred? The answer may be obvious, and we must admit to it.

What about fear? Are we afraid again? If so our inventory is no longer a fearless inventory. We must discover what we did wrong to permit fear and promptly admit to it.

The answer to all of these problems will be the same. The wrong we must admit to is that we violated the contract we made with God in the Third Step. When we turn our wills and our lives over to God's care, it naturally follows that we must accept what He gives us no matter what.

If we have become egotistical, it is because we are managing our own lives again or, at the very least, trying to take credit for self-management. We must admit this and turn our wills back over to the care of God.

If we have become greedy, it means we are not satisfied with what God has given us and are seeking by a return to self-management to grab more than He provides. If we can admit that, we can get back on His track.

Dishonesty means we are conspiring with our own ego to change His plans and utilizing man-created techniques of lying and cheating in an attempt to manage our lives rather than letting God manage them.

Self-pity is a clear breach of our contract with the Higher Power. We obviously do not live up to our agreement to accept whatever He gives us each day. Life is a series of pleasures held together by links of pain. God provides us with both the pleasures and the pain. Self-pity is obviously a result of not accepting both.

Resentment also means we are not gracefully accepting all that God gives us.

Envy means we are coveting the gifts of others rather than being grateful for our own.

Jealousy is also dissatisfaction with the way God is managing us.

Worry is caused by trying to plan the future rather than letting God plan it.

If we are angry, it is not because of other people's behavior. It is outrage at the way God is presenting them to us.

If we are depressed, so what? All we have to do is accept our depression as being part of God's plan and start wondering what great high the depression is leading to.

Hatred must mean we don't like whomever or whatever God has placed in our path. It means we are once again resisting the Will of God.

If there is fear in our inventory, it is because we

are responsible for what is in it instead of letting our Higher Power be responsible.

In other words, the wrong we must promptly admit to is not that we are angry, self-pitying, jealous, greedy or worrying. What we must admit is that we have repossessed our wills and our lives. To make ourselves well we must again and again, if necessary, turn one hundred percent of our wills and our lives over to the care of God. Anything less than that is the wrong we must promptly admit to.

All of our continuing defects of character indicate the same thing, a breach of our contract to fully accept the way He manages our lives. When we can admit that is our universal wrong, then we can let our Higher Power take command again.

Do we become vegetables waiting for God to happen to us? Not at all. We become the animals He created and wait for Him to make us act and react the way He intends us to. God obviously has no intention of making animals into vegetables. And man, His greatest and most versatile animal of all, can only reach ultimate fulfillment and activity in God's care.

Continuing to take daily inventory and promptly admitting when we are wrong must be done over and over in order to maintain the principles established by taking Steps One through Nine. Step Ten is a continuing test to see if we are adhering to Step Three. Are we really allowing our wills and our lives to remain in the care of God as we understand Him?

When we move on to the next Step, we do not abandon this one. We take it with us, and through it all the Steps before, as we go on to one of the most uplifting and gratifying Steps of all.

step eleven

Sought through prayer and meditation to improve our conscious contact with God *as we understood Him*, praying only for knowledge of His will for us and the power to carry that out.

THIS IS THE STEP WHERE WE EXperience our spiritual awakening. We may have thought we already were spiritually awakened because by the time we have progressed to this Step each of us will have had many spiritual experiences. For instance, many of you may have had a headache when you started reading this book but, after a few pages the headache was gone. And you took no aspirin to drive it away. Reading this spiritual book can actually eliminate a headache. Losing a headache in this manner is a spiritual experience.

Turning a problem over to the care of God may suddenly put a halt to our worry about the problem. Such sudden peace of mind is obviously a spiritual experience. But a spiritual experience is not a spiritual awakening. In fact, many spiritual experiences are required before a spiritual awakening is possible. It is only through experience that even the existence of a

Power Greater Than Ourselves is finally proven to us.

Spiritual awakening is when belief based on logic or blind faith is replaced by knowledge based on irrefutable evidence. Spiritual awakening is when we know, not believe, that there is a Power Greater Than Ourselves which has taken over the care of our wills and our lives, and that we can depend upon that Power to run the show from here on out.

Step Eleven reaffirms the contract we made with Him in Step Three when we first made the decision to turn our will and our lives over to God's care.

If you have not already established a conscious contact with your Higher Power, you cannot take the Eleventh Step. This Step is not to *establish* our conscious contact with God. It is to *improve* our conscious contact with Him.

We have already made a conscious contact with God at least three times in earlier Steps before we are ready by Step Eleven to improve our already existing conscious contact with Him. In Step Three we made a decision to turn our wills and our lives over to God's care. If we really decided to do this, we did it. And you can't turn anything at all, much less your will and your life, over to another entity without contacting it. The very act of turning your will and life over to God's care is a conscious contact with God.

In Step Five, we admitted something to God, to ourselves and to another human being. We admitted our wrongs directly to Him, even before we confessed to ourselves and to someone else. Such admission to other entities is direct conscious contact. You can't tell someone something without contacting that person. You can't admit anything to God without consciously contacting Him.

In Step Seven, we humbly asked Him to do something. We actually and consciously asked Him to remove our shortcomings and then held our egos to one side so He could take away our defects of character without our interference. You can't ask someone to do something, not even God, without consciously making contact.

So having established a conscious contact with God at least three times in Steps Three, Five and Seven, we now in Step Eleven seek to *improve* that contact, just as the verb suggests.

How? By prayer and meditation. In many nations of the world those who take this Step have been trained from the cradle to meditate, but may know little about how to pray. Others trained in Western religions will know how to pray, but many never have been taught to meditate.

To pray is to petition God for what you would like to have Him give you. It is to specify exactly what it is you would like to have Him provide for you, or for Him to at least help you obtain these things for yourself. We are all taught to pray for people, places and things. We pray for God to help us achieve physical, mental or spiritual goals, always being careful to spell out exactly what we want God to do for us. We pray for God to do our bidding. We try our best to make a servant out of God.

Meditation is just the opposite. There are many techniques of meditation such as counting backward in varicolored numbers, chanting mantras or rosaries, thinking of nothing at all, and so forth. All meditation techniques seek to do the same thing. They are designed to drive all everyday thoughts and concerns from our brains. The purpose of meditation is to empty our minds of all our own concerns and create a thought void into which the Creative Force, or God, may enter.

Prayer is to tell God what we want. Meditation is to listen to what God wants. The wrong kinds of prayer can be a form of black magic, for when we seek to use a supernatural force to help us achieve our goals, it ceases to be supernatural and becomes superhuman. To make God into a servant is to place Him under our superhuman power. Yet is this not exactly what we have long been taught to do? To get down on our knees and pray for God to go to work for us?

We have frequently been warned to *be careful what you pray for because you might get your wish*. Well that obligation of having to decide what to pray for in detail, like making up a shopping list for God, is removed by the Eleventh Step. We need never again worry about what to ask Him for. Step

Eleven tells us precisely the *only things we may pray for. In this Step of spiritual awakening we pray only for knowledge of His will for us and the power to carry that out.*

The word *only* is in there and it means from now on we pray for nothing else except His will and the courage to go ahead and do what He makes us want to do.

The miracle of this prayer, asking God for knowledge of His will and the power to carry that out, is that it ceases to become the kind of praying we are used to, and becomes in fact, its own form of meditation, whether we know how to meditate or not. Praying *only for His will and the power to carry that out* actually drives all our personal concerns from our consciousness and concentrates *only on His concerns*. That kind of prayer is meditation. The very prayer empties our mind of our own wants and allows God to enter.

How do we know His will? If we let Him, God creates everything, even our will. God creates our wants and our not-wants. All we have to do is carry out what He makes us want to do and not do what He makes us reject.

If we have thoroughly placed our will in His care and pray only for knowledge of His will and the power to carry that out, we must trust our will as being directed by Him. The power to carry it out will be the courage to do so, and He will give us that, too.

Think of it. If we *continue to take personal inventory* and promptly admit it every time we snatch our wills back from the care of God as we understand Him, we can go ahead and do everything He makes us want to do all the time. That means, if we stick to the principles of these Steps, we can always do what we want and never do what we don't want.

It is freedom so complete that society and those of us still conditioned by society will think there must be something wrong with it. For society by definition is a system of rules, customs, and regulations. And rules, customs and regulations, even those imposed in the impossible hope of preserving freedom, are the opposite of freedom. In true freedom there are no rules.

In the Twelve Steps there are none. It is only suggested that you turn your will and your life over to the care of God and *pray only for knowledge of His will for us and the power to carry that out*. It's not a rule. You don't have to do it unless you want to. But if you have completed Steps One through Ten, you will want to, because He will make you want to.

And please note, the Step does not suggest praying only for knowledge of His will *for you*, or that I pray only for knowledge of His will *for me*. It suggests we pray for His will *for us*. When He answers our prayer and meditation with that kind of knowledge, I will do nothing to hurt you, and you will quite naturally not do anything that would hurt me or anyone else.

We've got to trust God's will through our own or the whole program goes down the drain.

But when we take that gamble and follow the instincts He gives us over and over again, our rewards will be so great that we will indeed come to know, not merely believe, that there is a God, that He has taken charge, and that we can trust and depend upon Him to motivate us in everything we do.

Knowing God indeed is in charge of our lives and that He is managing us beautifully, is a spiritual awakening. Being glad we are exactly the way God created us and confident enough to daily bet our entire present and future on Him is a spiritual awakening. Discovering that by giving up to Him you become a sure winner in all you do is a spiritual awakening. God has many ways of letting you know He has taken back full responsibility for your life. You need not wonder how you can tell when it happens. When you awaken spiritually, you will know it.

And when you are spiritually awake, you will be ready to move on to the Twelfth Step.

step twelve

Having had a spiritual awakening as the result of these Steps, we tried to carry this message to others, and to practice these principles in all our affairs.

THIS STEP IS HOW WE STAY SPIRI- tually awake by telling others how we got this way. By practicing the principles of the Twelve Steps we achieve unquestionable success. And to keep it, we've got to give it away.

An absolute requirement for taking the Twelfth Step is that we have completed to the best of our ability, and God's, the Eleven Steps which precede this one. We must have already had a spiritual awakening in order to validly tell others how they, too, may achieve one. We must be in God's hands in order to extend the hand of God. We must be absolutely certain we have totally surrendered our wills and our lives to God's care. And we must be completely satisfied and in full acceptance of the results as He presents them to us one day at a time. We now must know there is no other time but now, that however our wills respond right now to what- ever He now presents us with is the way He wants us to respond. There will never be any other time but now, for now is all there is, and we accept whatever is happening to us now as part of God's gift of love.

We've got to be positive that a Spirit greater than ourselves is fully in charge of everything we say or do, and that we have by experience learned to implicitly trust that Greater Spirit to govern our conscious and unconscious lives. When we know at last that there is no boss but God, no supervisor other than the Higher Power and no inspiration other than that One Great Mover of our universe, then and only then can we proceed with the Twelfth Step.

We cannot carry the message to others until we are irrevocably convinced that there is no other road to success *and* happiness except total surrender of our minds and bodies to the care of God, for that *is* the first part of the message. The rest of the message is that the way to accomplish this miracle of giving up to win is to meticulously take each and every one of the Twelve Steps. And to deliver the message with any conviction at all, it must be obvious by the glowing examples of our spiritually awakened lives that we have already taken all Twelve Steps.

How do we carry the message? We voluntarily tell others how the Twelve Steps have transformed our own lives, going out of our way to share our miraculous experience with those in obvious need of help. We tell them what we used to be like, what happened when we took the Twelve Steps, and what we are like now.

We do not evangelize, nor seek converts. We merely deliver the message of the Twelve Steps. What those we deliver it to do about the message, whether they follow the Twelve suggested Steps or not, is entirely up to them. If they do not choose to travel our path, it is not our failure. We successfully delivered the message, whether those to whom we deliver it choose to listen or not to listen.

We may deliver the message by speaking to groups or by dropping it into casual conversation. We can tell the story in books, articles, on the dramatic stage in comedy or tragedy form, by means of TV and motion pictures, by letter, on signboards or in graffiti scribbled on a wall. We can tell it in the Hollywood Bowl, the Superdome or in the third seat from the rear in a near empty bus. It matters not where or when we carry the message, nor how. Yet the most effective way to let others know what the Twelve Steps have to offer is by the gleaming examples of our own miraculously transformed lives.

We do this not by striving to achieve the stereotyped images of sainthood, sterling citizenship or material achievement, but rather by simply being ourselves the way God created us. The definition of success is to do what you want to do. The definition of failure is to not do what you want to do. By leaving it up to God to create our wants, others will notice that we always seem to be doing what we want to do, that obviously we are successful in our lives. And how could we fail to be happy doing what we want to all the time?

So we tell others about the Twelve Steps and show them by our own happy, successful way of living that they work.

And we continue to try to practice these principles in all our affairs:

We continue to admit our lives have become unmanageable. Not your life, nor mine, but *all our* lives are unmanageable.

We continue to believe that a Power greater than ourselves can restore us to sanity.

We keep on turning our wills and our lives over to the care of God whether we understand Him or not.

We continue to take personal inventory, and promptly admit to God, to ourselves and to another human being when we have wrongly wrested the management of our lives away from God's care.

We never stop humbly asking God to remove our shortcomings.

We always make direct amends to persons we have harmed, unless to do so would injure them or others.

We daily seek to improve our conscious contact with God by prayer and meditation, and the *only* way we now pray is for God's will for *us* and the power to carry that out.

And we keep right on telling others about all this so we can share with them some of the joy and well-being we have found. This will come naturally because by now we will have learned God's greatest secret. The greatest pleasure lies in giving others pleasure. So by carrying the wonderful message of the Twelve Steps to others and practicing the principles in all our affairs, we will be receiving that amount of joy into our own lives in direct ratio to the amount of pleasure we give away. And we will be receiving it from God.

That is the message. That is how it works. The rest is up to you and to God.

getting started

IT IS $TIME$ NOW TO GO $BACK$ TO Step One and see if you can take it. You can go it alone, or it may be easier if you get together to share experiences with others dedicated to the principles of the Twelve Steps. The best model for such a discussion group might be Alcoholics Anonymous who first discovered the Twelve Steps now successfully used by so many others who have problems other than alcohol.

If you find others who want to try the Twelve Steps as a group, try not to elect any regular officers other than rotating discussion chairpersons and perhaps a secretary to set up an agreed upon meeting place, provide refreshments and handle self-supporting contributions from group members to meet incidental expenses.

It is more difficult for an individual to be in constant contact with a Higher Power than for a group. A group works something like a chain letter. Invariably someone in the group is in contact with

THE TWELVE STEPS TO HAPPINESS

God so the rest of the members can latch on. In a group you can learn by sharing your mistakes as well as your successes with each other.

Or it can be done alone. I once met a man in Tahiti who was the only one deliberately trying to practice the Twelve Steps in fifty-thousand square miles of ocean and south sea islands. Ten years later we met again and compared how the Steps were working for him without a group in the South Pacific and for me where there were a thousand groups meeting weekly in the bay area of San Francisco. Both of us were happier, healthier and more prosperous than we had ever imagined we could be.

So the Twelve Steps work no matter how you take them, as long as you take them.

If you need advice about the Twelve Steps, ask any one of the millions of members of Smokers Anonymous, Overeaters Anonymous, Schizophrenics Anonymous, Narcotics Anonymous, Emotions Anonymous, Compulsive Sexuals Anonymous, Parents Anonymous, Mistresses Anonymous, Debtors Anonymous, the grandaddy of all self-help groups, Alcoholics Anonymous or any other anonymous group of losers that have become winners.

We all practice the same Twelve Steps. If they work for people with those kinds of problems, they'll work for you.

You don't have to be a loser to become a winner. All you have to do is take the Twelve Steps to happiness and success.

insta-step guide

I. *Admitted we were powerless, and that our lives had become unmanageable.*
   1. Admit you are powerless over your most difficult problem.
      a. Acknowledge it is useless to try to control it.
   2. Admit you cannot manage anything else.
      a. Recognize it is hopeless to try.
II. *Came to believe that a Power greater than ourselves could restore us to sanity.*
   1. Recognize that still trying to control what can't be managed is insane.
   2. Let yourself believe there *might be* a Power greater than you in the universe.
      a. Be willing to gamble that a Higher Power *might* make you sane enough to stop trying to manage.
III. *Made a decision to turn our will and our*

lives over to the care of God as we understood Him.

1. Gamble everything you are that a Higher Power will take charge of every aspect of your life.

   a. Take a chance. Turn your body, mind, spirit, and all your affairs over to the Great Unknown that might not even be there.

2. Address God directly. Say, "God, take charge!"

IV. *Made a searching and fearless moral inventory of ourselves.*

1. Remember an inventory is not a history. It's what's in stock now.

2. Examine your current behavior.

   a. What's good about yourself?

   b. What's defective?

   c. Ignore the past except for guilt, resentment, hatred or unforgiveness.

3. Write it all down, both good and bad.

4. If there is fear in your inventory it is not *fearless*.

   a. Put God back in charge.

   b. With God in charge, there's nothing to fear.

5. Take the inventory again without fear.

V. *Admitted to God, to ourselves and to an-*

other human being the exact nature of our wrongs. -

   1. Analyze what is causing each defect of character you found in Step Four.

      a. Why do you do such things?

      b. Do you trust yourself to handle your problems more than you trust God?

      c. Is *the nature of* your *wrongs* that you take control away from God?

   2. Admit to yourself, your Higher Power, and to someone else that you keep trying to manage an unmanageable life because you don't trust God to do it for you.

VI. *Were entirely ready to have God remove all these defects of character.*

   1. Step Six has already happened to you if you are ready to *let God* remove your shortcomings.

      a. If you insist on working on your own defects instead of letting your Higher Power eliminate them, repeat Steps Four and Five until you acquire enough humility to *let God remove them His way in His Own Time.*

VII. *Humbly asked Him to remove our shortcomings.*

   1. Speak to God. Ask Him to take away

all character defects, even those not
listed.

    a. Be humble enough to *let Him.*

VIII. *Made a list of all persons we had harmed
and became willing to make amends to them
all.*

    1. List every person you ever harmed,
and the damage you did to them.

        a. Include those you think *had it
coming to them.*

    2. Remember an amend is more than an
apology. It is compensation for actual
damage.

    3. Become willing to make restitution to
every person on the list.

        a. At this point, eliminate no one
from your list for any reason.
That comes later.

IX. *Made direct amends to such people wherever possible, except when to do so would
injure them or others.*

    1. Seek out those we damaged.

        a. Eliminate those our amends
would harm further.

        b. Eliminate amends that might
damage an accomplice.

        c. Do nothing that would hurt any-
one else.

        d. Don't worry about those whom

you can't find. You may run into them later.

    e. If it's impossible to make amends now, do it later if it becomes possible.

    f. Forget about amends you can never make.

    g. Take your own name off the list. You are making amends to yourself by taking these Steps.

2. Correct the damage you did to those still on the list.

    a. Apology isn't enough. Make appropriate physical, mental, emotional, or financial restitution for each harm you caused.

X. *Continued to take personal inventory, and when we were wrong, promptly admitted it.*

1. Each day examine your feelings and behavior.

    a. It's a spot check. You may have neither time nor need to write it down.

    b. What are you doing or thinking that is making you uncomfortable?

2. What's the nature behind what's wrong?

    a. Is it because you don't trust God to handle something?

      b. Are *you* trying to manage it?

   3. Admit you have grabbed control from your Higher Power.

   4. Do Step Three. Put God back in charge.

XI. *Sought through prayer and meditation to improve our conscious contact with God, as we understood Him, praying only for knowledge of His will for us, and the power to carry that out.*

   1. Reestablish the conscious contact previously established in Steps Three, Five, and Seven.

      a. Directly address God.

   2. Meditate to empty your mind of all personal concerns.

      a. Get your mind totally off yourself. Get your ego out of the way so the Creative Force may fill your brain with new thoughts and intuition.

      b. Set no goals for meditation.

      c. Leave what follows to God.

   3. From now on pray *only* for knowledge of God's will and the power to carry it out.

      a. Never pray for anything else.

      b. Address God. Say, "God, make me feel like doing *only what you want me to do*. Make me feel like not doing anything you don't want me to do.''

4. Now do what you feel like doing. You prayed *for the power to carry it out.*

   a. Trust the intuition you asked your Higher Power to create.

5. You are spiritually awake when you trust God in all things without telling Him what to do.

XII. *Having had a spiritual awakening as the result of these steps, we tried to carry this message to others, and to practice these principles in all our affairs.*

1. You are spiritually awake *as the result* of taking Steps One through Nine.

   a. You no longer list things for God to do.

   b. You have abandoned yourself to God's unpredictable management.

   c. You accept what happens, good or bad, as part of His plan.

2. Explain the Twelve Steps to others who seek happiness and success.

3. Practice Twelve Step principles in everything you do.

About the Author

Retired Air Force Lt. Colonel Joe Klaas, M.A., has authored seven books in English and two in Dutch, including the popular recovery book, TWELVE TRADITIONS FOR ALL OF US, and has recorded TWELVE STEPS: THE ROAD TO RECOVERY, SERENITY AND HAPPINESS, a classic audio cassette album.

Klaas served as an American volunteer Spitfire pilot in the R.A.F., and has won twenty British and American decorations. He has also been a radio newscaster and an A.P. correspondent. He has been a guest on dozens of talk shows and conducted seminars for counselors, psychotherapists, medical doctors and patients from coast to coast.

"EASY DOES IT, BUT DO IT"
with Hazelden RecoveryBooks

THE 12 STEPS TO HAPPINESS *by Joe Klaas*

345-36787-1 $5.99

BARRIERS TO INTIMACY: For People Torn by Addiction and Compulsive Behavior *by Gayle Rosellini and Mark Worden*

345-36735-9 $4.99

BACK FROM BETRAYAL: Recovering from His Affairs *by Jennifer P. Schneider, M.D.* 345-36786-3 $4.95

LIVING RECOVERY: Inspirational Moments for 12 Step Living *by Men and Women in Anonymous Programs*

345-36785-5 $4.99

COMPULSIVE EATERS AND RELATIONSHIPS *by Aphrodite Matsakis, Ph.D.* 345-36831-2 $4.99

SHOWING UP FOR LIFE: A Recovering Overeater's Triumph over Compulsion *by Heidi Waldrop*

345-37379-0 $4.99

These bestsellers are available in your local bookstore, or order by calling toll free 1-800-733-3000 to use your major credit card.

Prices and order numbers subject to change without notice. Valid in the U.S. only.

For information about the Hazelden Foundation, its books, and its treatment and professional services call 1-800-328-9000. Outside the U.S. call (612) 257-4010.